# JOKES *for* KIDS
## BOOK

AF225013

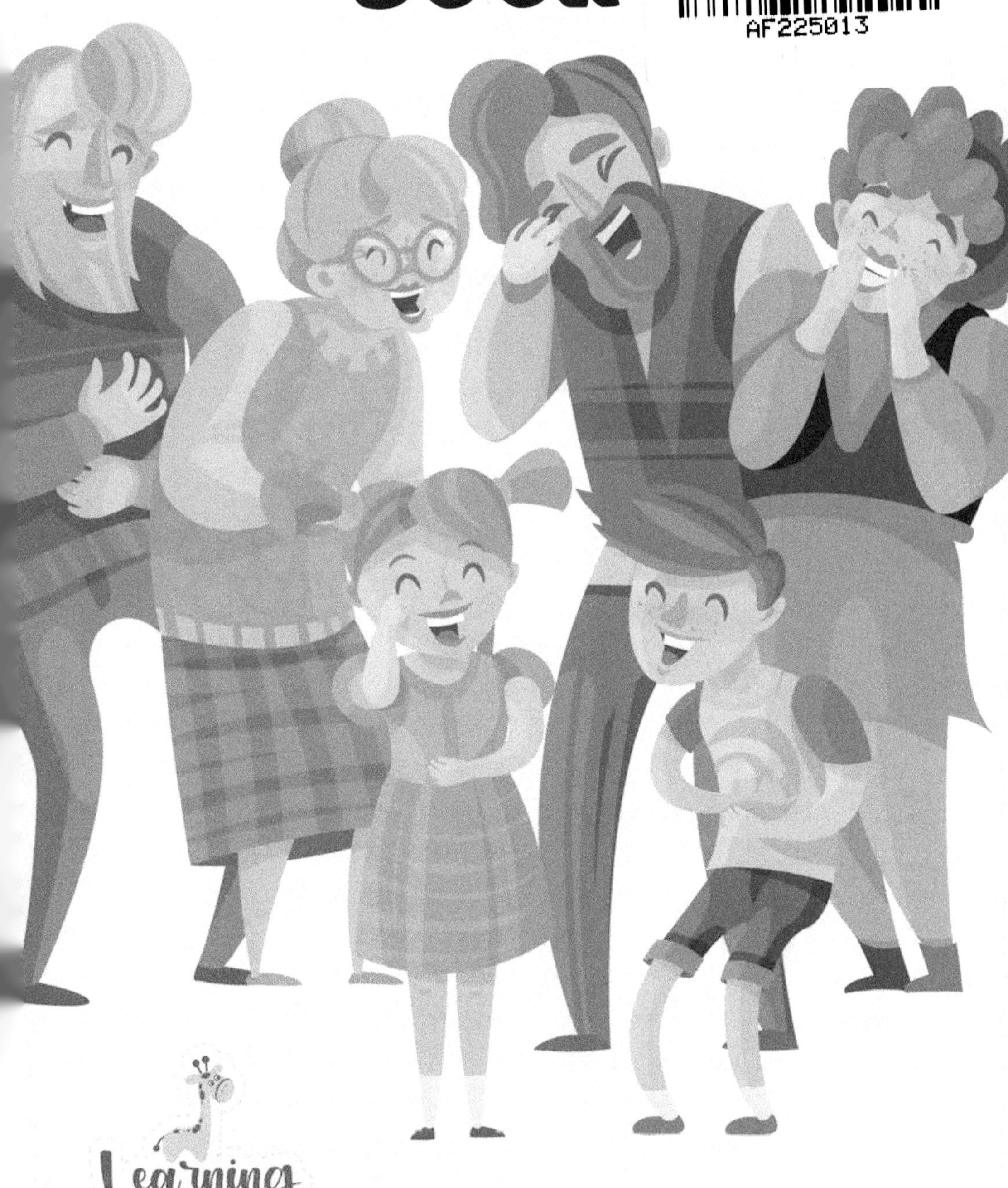

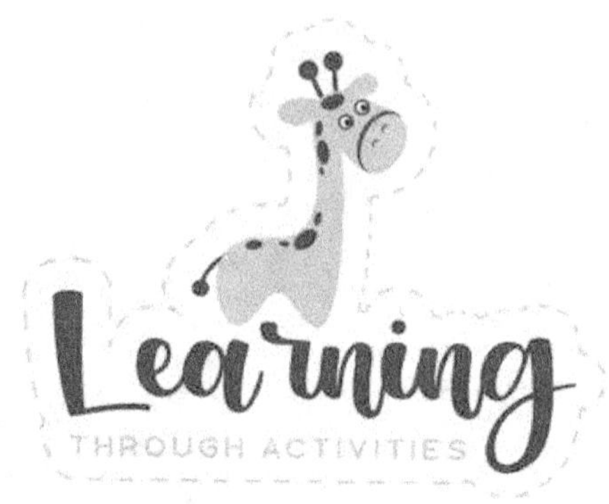
Learning
THROUGH ACTIVITIES

# JOKES for KIDS BOOK

Laughter is the best medicine, and there's nothing better than making your friends and family laugh with a good joke. Sharing a good laugh is a great way to socialize, and joking around with your helps build your bond and relationship. But it can be difficult to come up with jokes on the spot, hey? Especially if you aren't used to being a funny person.

If you really enjoy making your friends laugh, but you are struggling to come up with jokes, then you've picked up the right book! We've got hundreds of jokes within these pages for you to tell your friends, family, pets, and furniture. So, warm up your vocal cords and get your cheeky face on because you're about to become the comedian of your dreams.

We've organized these jokes into various categories for your convenience, from things like animal jokes, family jokes, dinosaur jokes, and more. If you're looking to improve your joking game, then keep on reading!

# WHO TO TELL
## *your jokes to*

Do not waste your jokes with those who would never appreciate them It hurts to tell a good joke, and nobody laughs! Below are those you should tell your jokes to:

**Your pet** - if it can laugh out loud.
**Yourself** - six times a day.
**Mom** - whether she's mad at you or not.
**Dad** - whether you've been a good kid or not.
**Granny** - whether or not you've been a good grandchild.
**Any other person that wishes you well.**

**Key:** What if they don't laugh at your jokes? Use your fingers to tickle them! You have the right!

# WHO NOT TO TELL
## *your jokes to*

**A sleeping donkey.**
**Yourself** - after having bad grades in school.
**Granny** - who's feeling sleepy.
**Mom** - on a phone call with her boss.
**Dad** - who's looking for his misplaced money and who's suspecting you.

Therefore, tell your jokes to the
RIGHT PERSON; do it at the
RIGHT TIME and in the RIGHT PLACE.

# Table of
# CONTENTS


ANIMAL JOKES                6

DINOSAUR JOKES             24

FOOD JOKES                 37

SPACE JOKES                47

DOCTOR JOKES               58

KNOCK KNOCK JOKES          62

CORNY JOKES                78

CROSS THE ROAD JOKES       89

MUSIC JOKES                94

SCHOOL JOKES               97

BIRTHDAY JOKES            106

BONUS JOKES               116

RIDDLES                   119

PUNS                      127

# ANIMAL
## Jokes

Don't you just love hearing a joke or a moral story that has to do with animals? Yep, kids love animals, but do animals love them back? Of course they do! Here is a very special list of animal jokes for kids:

Q: Why do dogs bark?

A: Because they can't hiss like snakes.

Q: Where should you never take a turkey to?
A: Christmas party!

Q: Which bird is a carpenter?
A: A Woodpecker.

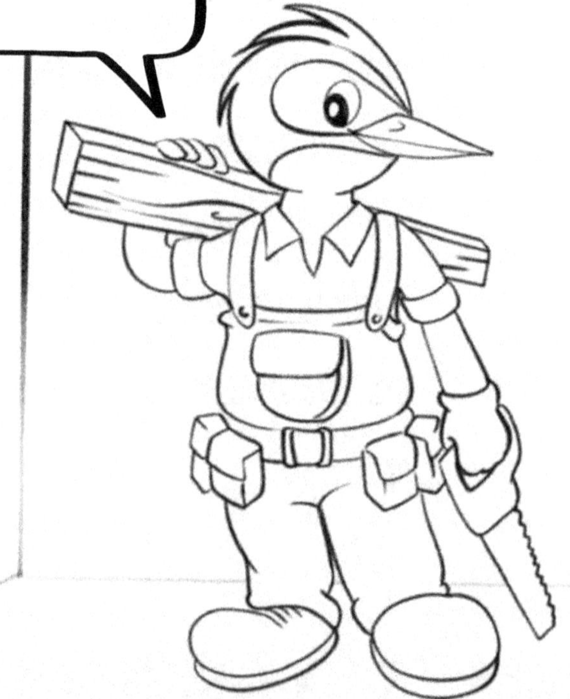

**Q: Why would a dog chew your dictionary?**
**A: To be able to speak out the words.**

**Q: If an ant becomes an elephant's friend, how do they communicate?**
**A: The ant has to live in the elephant's ears.**

**Q. Why does the monkey enter the anaconda's mouth?**
**A: It's visiting its parents and grandparents.**

**Q: What happens if rats suddenly become lions?**
**A: Cats would migrate to another world.**

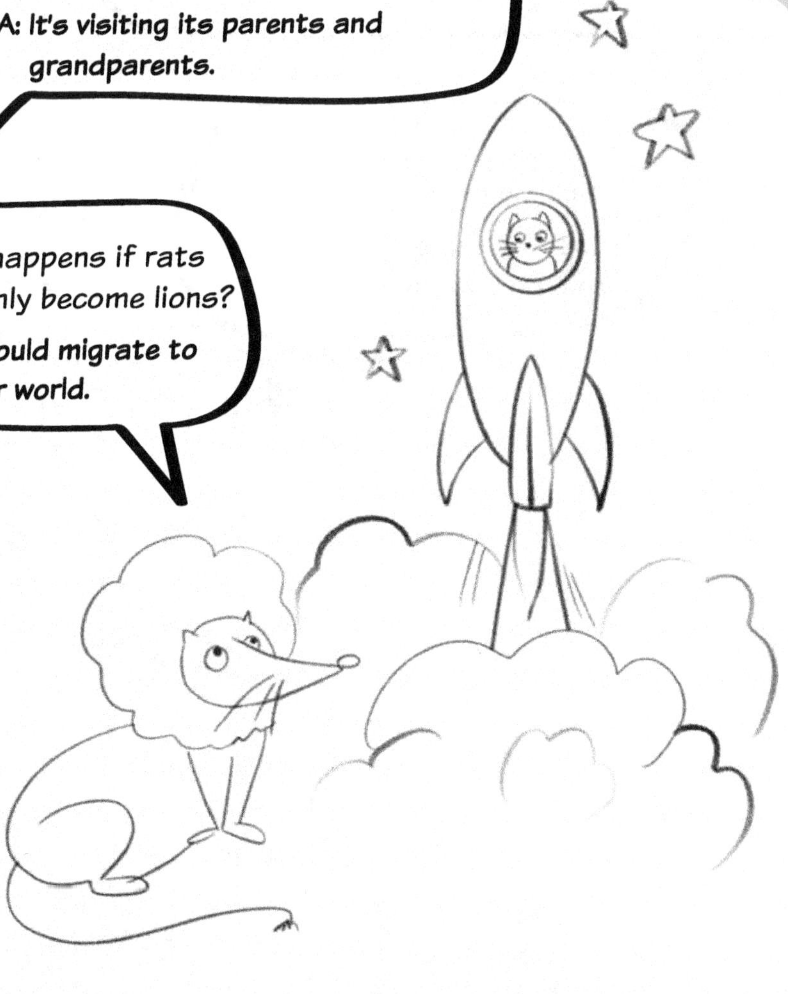

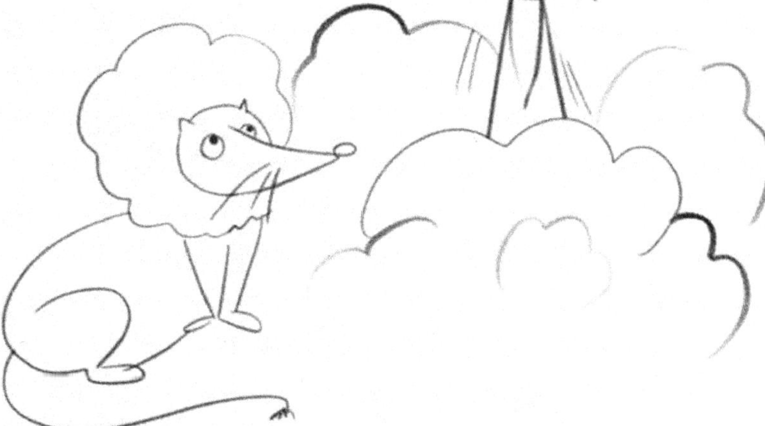

Q: What does being a 'bald eagle' mean?

A: Being a prominent elder.

Q: Why does the spider spend so much time weaving its webs?

A: Because it hates to chase its prey around like other unwise animals.

Q: Why do camels have humps on their backs?

A: Because their parents had it.

Q: How did the butterfly become so beautiful?

A: Because she sold her ugliness to Mrs. Caterpillar.

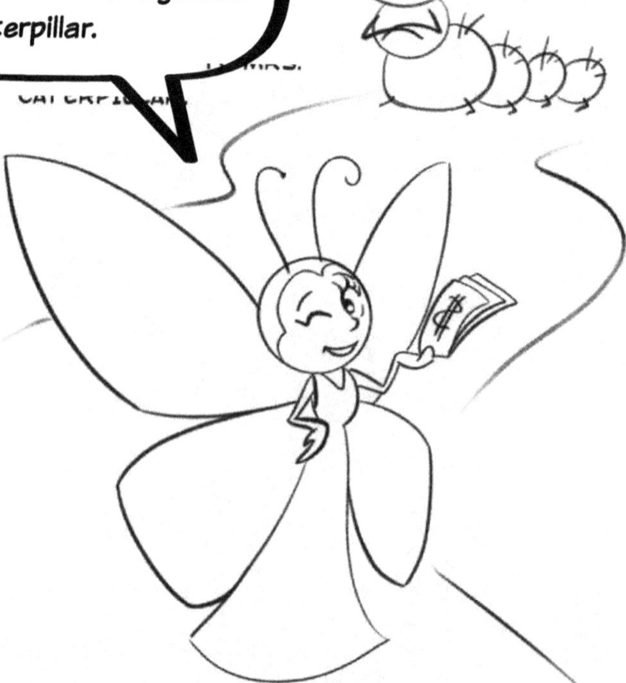

12. Q: Are cats and catfish truly related?

A: Well, they were twin sisters until the ocean came and adopted one.

Q: Why do rats run away from cobras?

A: Because they don't want to visit the cobra's stomach.

Q: Who does the cricket sing to every night?

A: Himself.

Q: Should a lion pity on a handicapped deer?

A: Yes, if the lion is not too hungry.

Q: What do you call a flying dragon?

A: Dragonfly.

Q: Which of the lizard is a company supervisor?

A: Monitor lizard.

Q: Why do fish live in saltwater?

A: Because pepper would kill them!

Q: When does a monkey hate its long tail?

A: When the lion nearly caught it by the tail.

Q: Which type of bug applies makeup?

A: Ladybug.

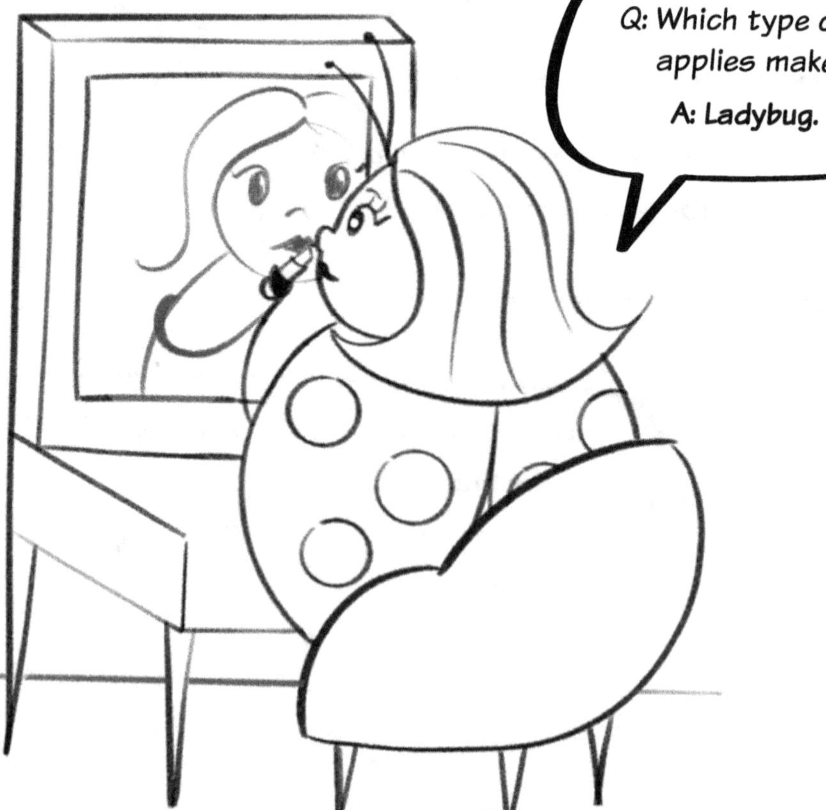

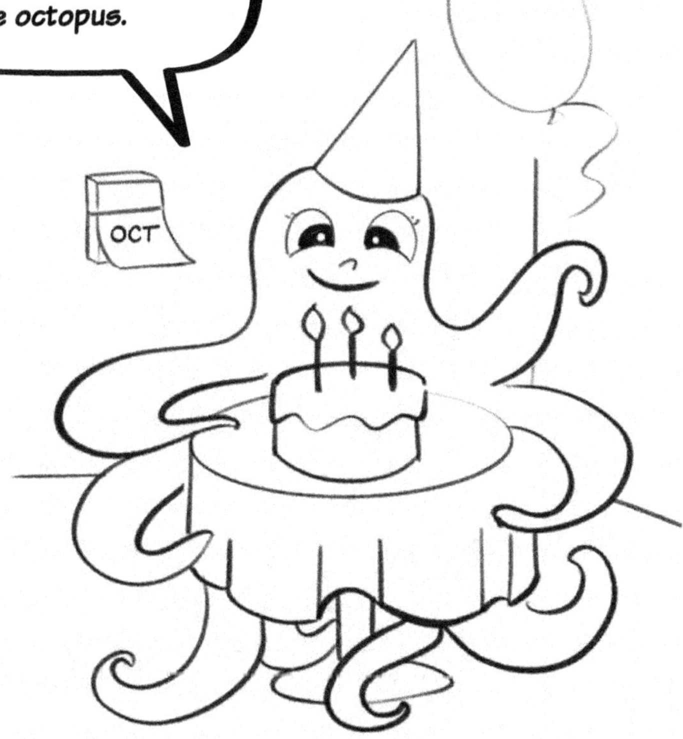
Q: How do you know that mosquitoes are good singers?
A: When they pass by your ears.
Q: What do you call a goat on the mountain?
A: Mountain goat.
Q: Why are the rats partying in the sitting room?
A: Because the new cat is blind.
Q: Which animal is only born in October?
A: The octopus.
OCT

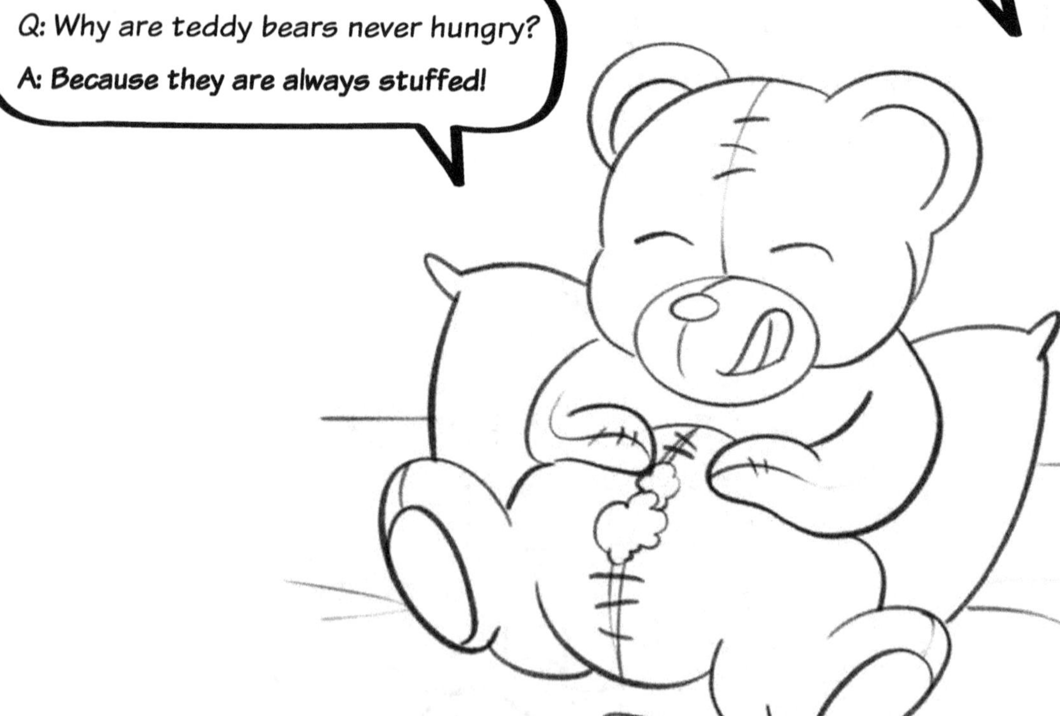

Q: Which lion won the swimming competition?
A: Sealion.

Q: What's a sleeping bull called?
A: A bulldozer.

Q: What will you call a cow that has no milk?
A: An udder failure.

Q: Why do gorillas have oversized nostrils?
A: Because they have oversized fingers!

Q: Why are teddy bears never hungry?
A: Because they are always stuffed!

Q: What did the judge say when the skunk walked into the courtroom?
A: Odor in the court!

Q: Why are fish so smart?
A: Because they live in schools.

Q: What instrument does an elephant play?
A: Trumpet.

Q: How do lions greet other animals in the jungle?
A: Pleased to eat you.

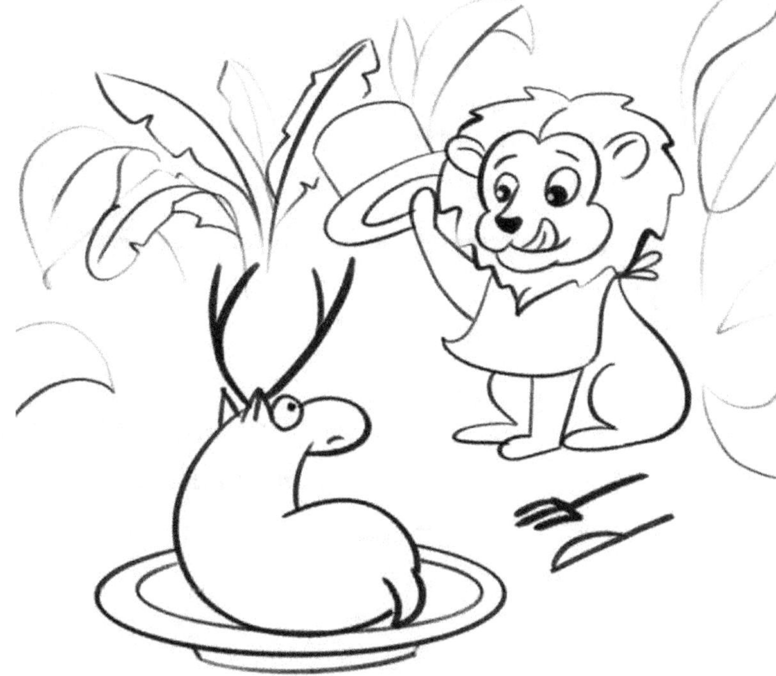

Q: What did the lion say after eating a comedian?

A: That human tasted funny!

Q: Which particular fish only swim at night?

A: A starfish!

Q: Why is a fish easy to weigh?

A: Because it has its own scales!

Q: What animals appear on legal documents?

A: Seals!

Q: What do you get when you cross a snake and a pie?

A: A pie-thon!

Q: What on earth is 'out of bounds'?

A: An exhausted kangaroo!

Q: What do you call a bear that has no ears?

A: 'B!'

Q: Why are elephants so wrinkled?

A: Because they don't iron their skins!

Q: Which day does an elephant sit on the fence?

A: The day to fix the fence!

Q: By what means do bees get to school?

A: By school buzz!

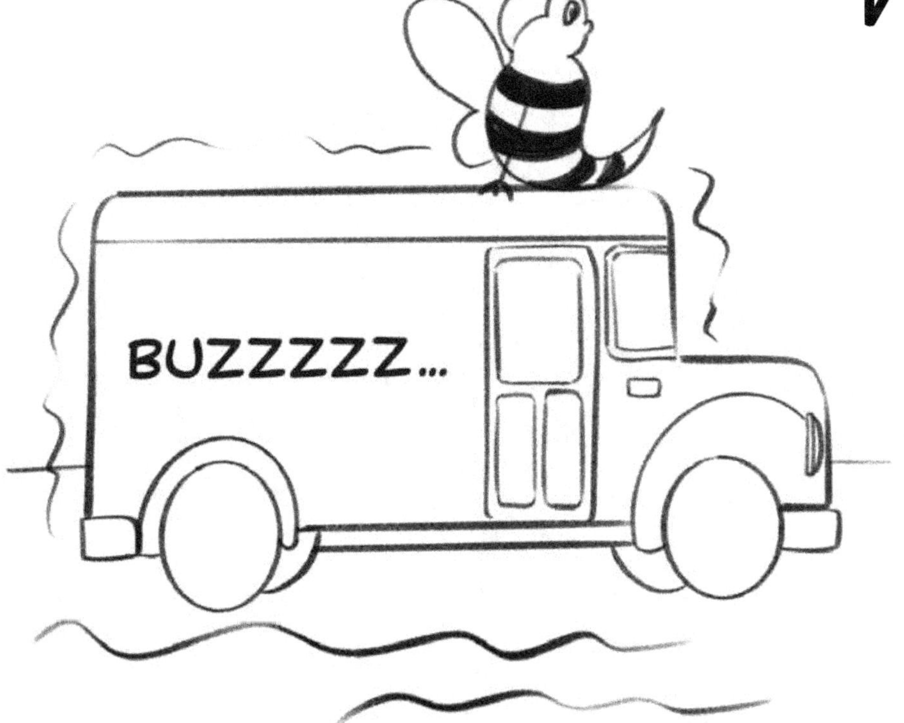

Q: How does an elephant communicate with his family in another country?

A: On the elephone!

Q: Where do fish keep their savings?

A: In a river-bank!

Q: What do you call a fish with no eyes?

A: 'Fsh!'

Q: How do prawns and clams talk to each other?

A: With shell-phones!

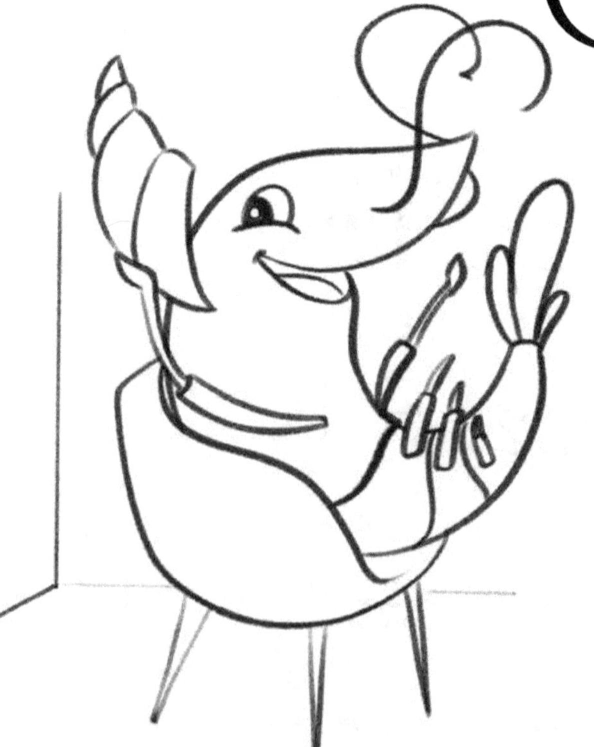

Q: What do you call a fish with a suit and tie?

A: SoFISHticated.

Q: How do you make an octopus laugh?

A: With ten-tickles.

Q: What do you call a bird that's afraid to fly?

A: A chicken.

Q: Why do rabbits run in circles?

A: Because it's hard to run in squares!

Q: What happens when you cross a dog and a calculator?

A: A friend you can count on.

Q: What is a dog's favorite instrument?

A: Trombone.

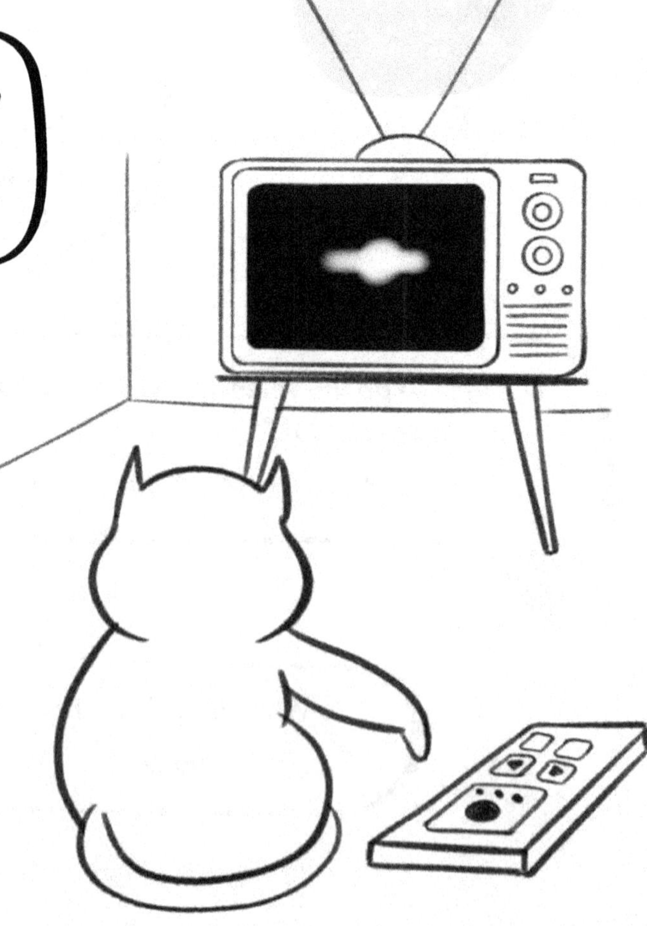
Q: Why did the dog chase its own tail?
A: To make ends meet.
Q: What happens when you try to cross a pit bull with a computer?
A: You get a lot of bites!
Q: Why is a tree like a big dog?
A: They both have a lot of bark!
Q: How did the cat stop a TV show?
A: He pressed paws!

Q: What was the dog's opinion at the meeting?

A: Nothing, he was barking the whole time.

Q: What's a dog's preferred dinner?

A: Pooched eggs.

Q: What do cows use to count?

A: A cowculator!

Q: Where do cows visit on holidays?

A: The moo-vies!

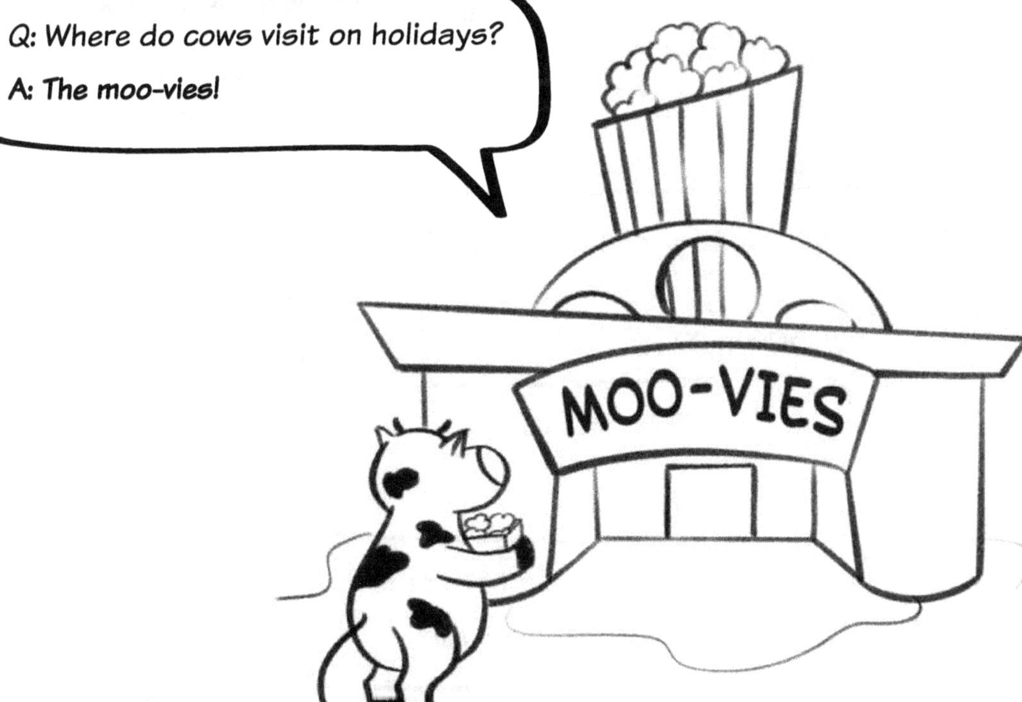

Q: Why can't you tell a cow secrets?

A: Because they'll tell the udders!

Q: Where can you find out more about cows?

A: Mooseum.

Q: What music do cows like to dance to?

A: Reggae MOOsic!

Q: Why was the cow terrified?

A: He was a cow-herd.

Q: What do you call two horses living next door?

A: Neigh-bors.

Q: What's a horse's favorite sport?

A: Stable tennis.

Q: Where do horses go when they fall sick?

A: Horse-pital!

Q: Why did the horse sail on a boat?

A: He was in the Neigh-vy!

Q: Which kind of horse can jump higher than a house?

A: Every horse – houses don't jump!

Q: Why did the horse cross the road?

A: Somebody shouted 'Hay!'

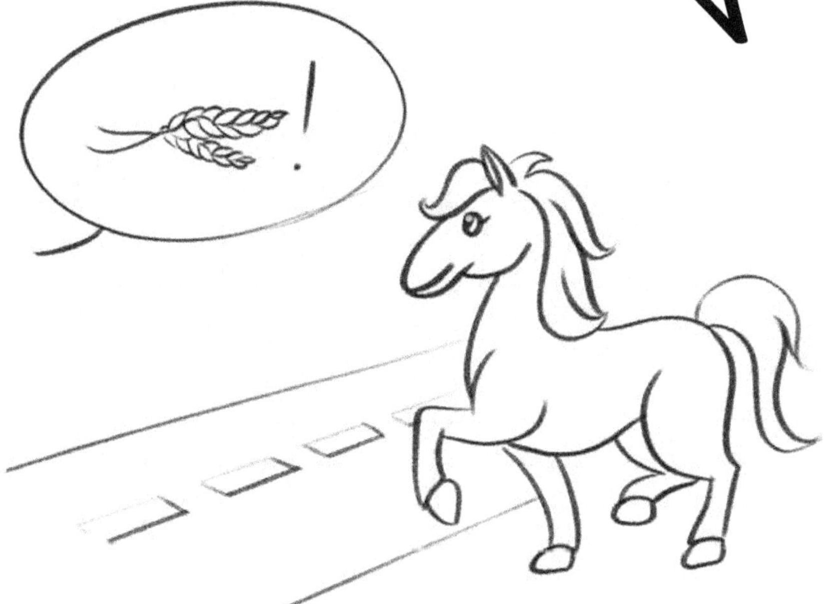

Q: Which illness do horses fear the most?

A: Hayfever!

Q: How do you fit more pigs on your farm?

A: Build a sty-scraper!

Q: What does a pampered cow give you?

A: Spoiled milk.

Q: What sound do porcupines make when they kiss?

A: Ouch!

Q: Where do polar bears go to vote?

A: The North Poll.

Q: What do you call cows that won't produce milk?

A: Milk duds!

Q: Why did the snake cross the road?

A: To get to the other sssssssside.

Q: What do you call a chicken that lays eggs on a slope?

A: An eggroll!

79. Q: What did the buffalo say to her son when he went away?

A: Bison!

80. Q: Why didn't the girl believe the tiger?

A: She thought it was a lion!

# DINOSAUR
## Jokes

Dinosaurs were one of the most adventurous and intelligent animals on Earth. They are fascinating, that's why kids love them. Below is the list of dinosaur jokes to crack your ribs!

Q: How do you know there's a dinosaur in your fridge?

A: The door won't shut!

Q: If Harry Potter were a dinosaur, who would he be?

A: The Dinosorcerer.

Q: What is the name of a sleeping dinosaur?

A: A dino-snore!

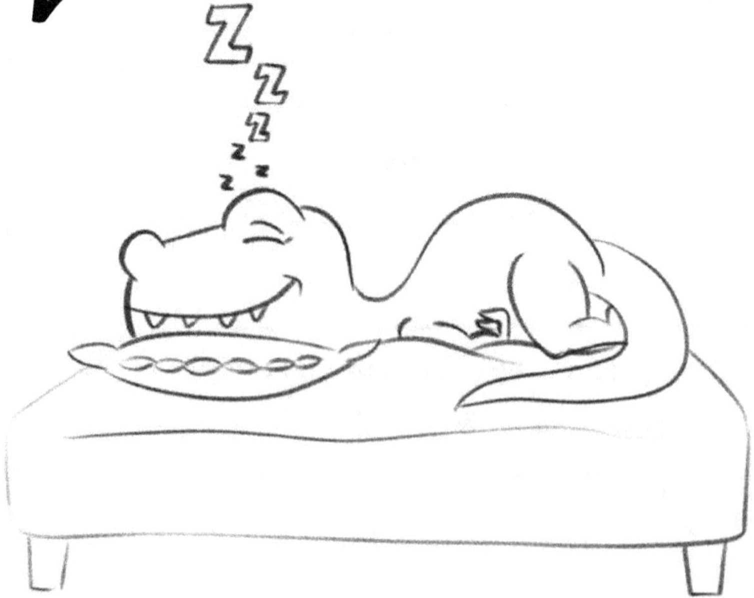

Q: What do dinosaurs eat with steak?

A: Dinosauce.

Q: What makes the Stegosaurus a good volleyball player?

A: He knows how to spike the ball!

Q: What's behind a dinosaur?

A: Its tail!

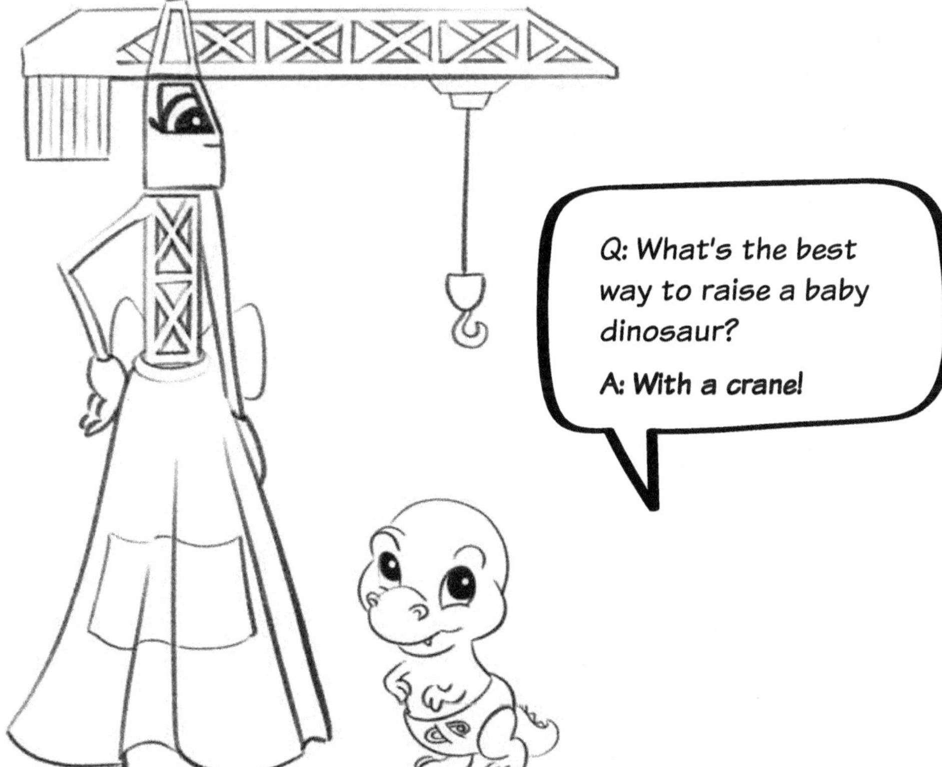

Q: Where does a triceratops sit?

A: It's tricera-bottom.

Q: What do you find on the kitchen floors of dinosaurs?

A: Rep-tiles.

Q: What do you call a person who puts their right hand in a T-Rex's mouth?

A: A Lefty!

Q: What should you do if you see a Tyrannosaurus Rex?

A: Pray that it doesn't notice you.

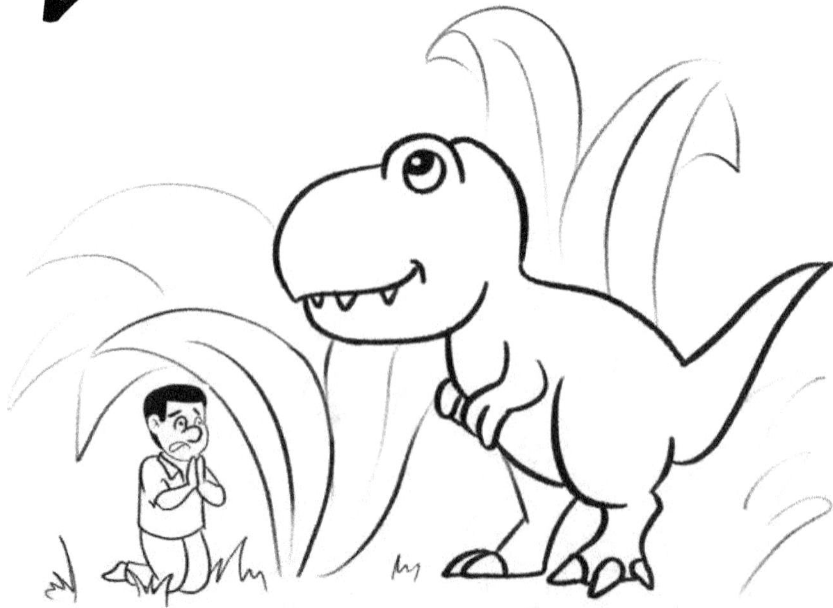

Q: What does the Brontosaurus like to do with humans?

A: Play Squash!

Q: Why did the dinosaur cross the road?

A: To eat the chickens on the other side.

Q: What does a dinosaur drink?

A: Tea-Rex.

Q: What does a carpenter dinosaur use?

A: A dino-saw.

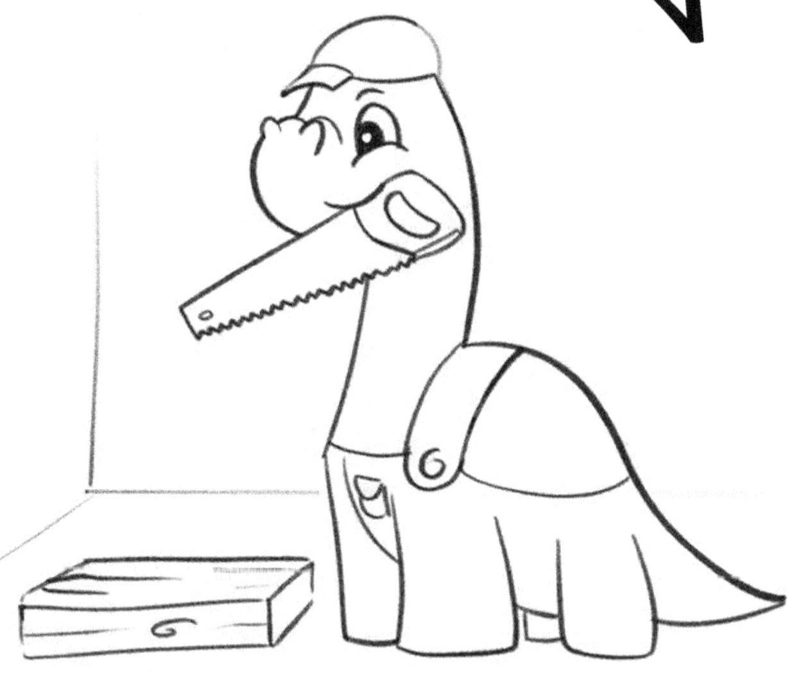

Q: What do you call a cowboy dinosaur?

A: Tyrannosaurus Tex!

Q: What made the Archaeopteryx catch the worm?

A: It was an early bird!

Q: Where do dinosaurs shop?

A: The dino-store!

Q: What do you call a T.Rex who hates losing?

A: A saur loser.

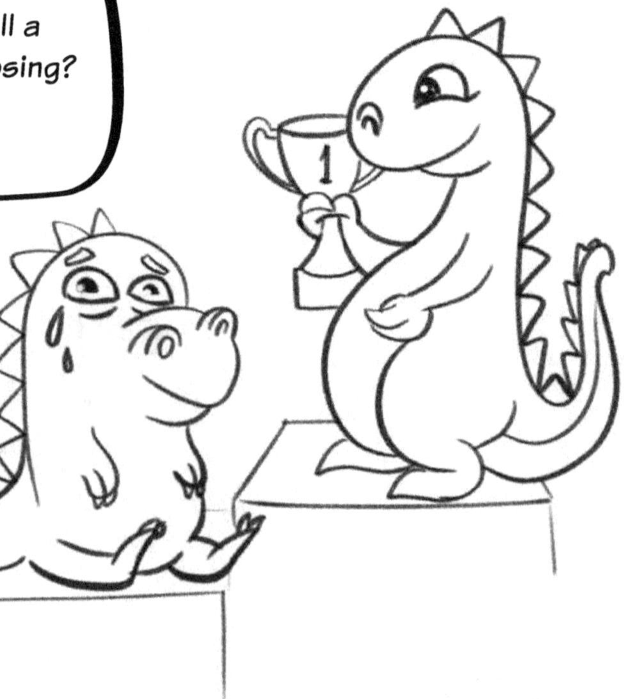

Q: What do you call the baby of a dinosaur and a pig?

A: Jurassic Pork!

Q: What's the name of twin dinosaurs?

A: Pair-odactyls!

Q: What do you call a dinosaur who left his sword out in the rain?

A: A **Stegosau-rust.**

Q: Why doesn't a Pterodactyl make any sound in the toilet?

A: Because the pee is silent!

Q: What do you think could tricera-top these dinosaur jokes?

A: I wish I knew, but I dino.

Q. What happens when a dinosaur crashes its car?

A: A Tyrannosaurus wreck!

Q: What name do you give a dinosaur choir?

A: A tyranno-chorus.

Q: What's a baby dinosaur called?

A: A Wee-Rex!

Q: What does a dinosaur call their girlfriend after they break up?

A: Tyrannosaurus Ex.

Q: What's a dinosaurs fart called?

A: An exstinktion!

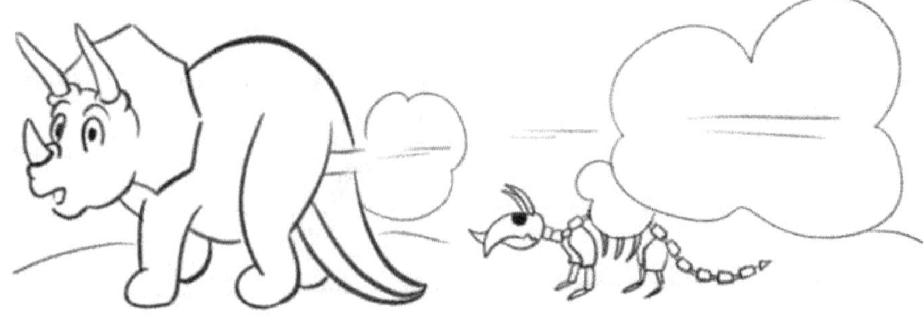

Q: What does a dinosaur use to blow stuff up?

A: Dino-mite!

Q: What's the ghost of a dinosaur called?

A: A **scaredactyl**.

Q: What does a short spiky dinosaur say when he falls down the stairs?

A: Ankle-is-sore-us!

Q: What did the dinosaur tell the cashier to do?

A: He asked him to keep the climate change.

Q: A dinosaur once said...

A: "Jurassic times call for Jurassic measures!"

Q: Why do they keep dinosaur bones in the museum?

A: Because they can't get new ones!

Q: What do you say when you see a dinosaur with one eye?

A: Do-you-think-he-saurus rex.

Q: Which dinosaur scares you the most?

A: A Terror-dactyl.

Q: Which dinosaur knows the most words?

A: A thesaurus!

Q: Which dinosaur gets anxious?

A: A nervous Rex.

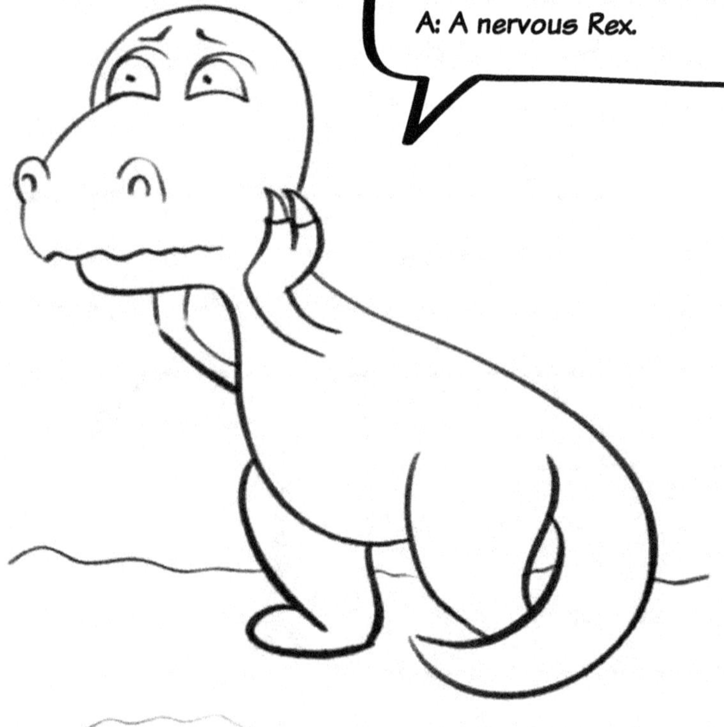

Q: What dinosaur snores a lot?

A: A Tyranno-snorus!

Q: How should you communicate with a Velociraptor?

A: Long-distance!

Q: What powered dinosaur cars?

A: Fossil fuels.

Q: Why did T-Rex's girlfriend cry?

A: Because she said he only loved her "this much" (with his tiny arms spread wide).

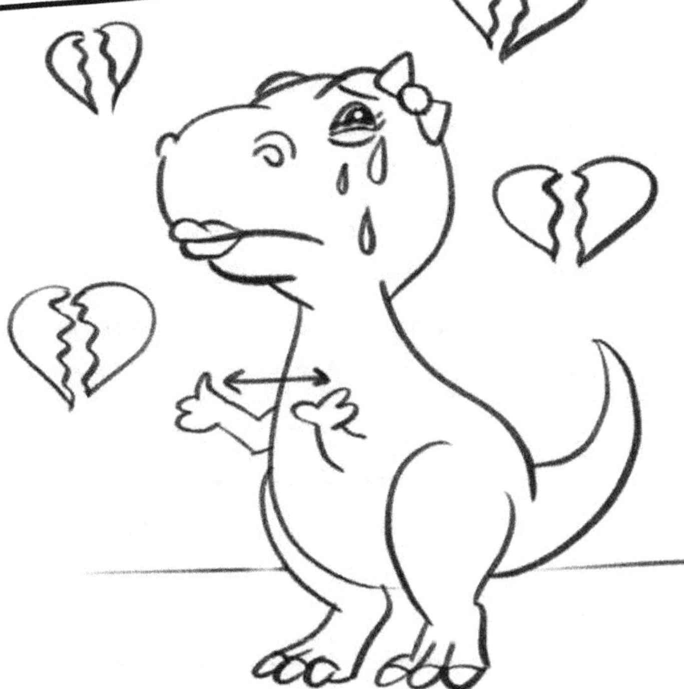

Q: Which dinosaur is fun to ride at a rodeo?

A: A Bronco-saurus!

Q: What are dinosaur fireworks called?

A: DINOMITE!

Q: What number does a T. Rex like the most?

A: Eight!

Q: Receptionist: Doctor, an invisible dinosaur is waiting to see you.

A: Doctor: Well, I can't see her!

Q: Why can't you hear dinosaurs go to the bathroom?

A: Because none of them are alive.

Q: Why did cavemen survive when the asteroid killed all of the dinosaurs?

A: Because they practiced social distancing by staying 56 million years apart.

Q: What dinosaur asks so many deep and meaningful questions?

A: A philosiraptor.

Q: What happens when a dinosaur sneezes?

A: You must get out of the way!

Q: What is noisier than a dinosaur?

A: Two dinosaurs!

Q: What do you say to a Stegosaurus that has carrots in its ears?

A: Whatever you want, it won't hear you at all!

Q: How would you feel if a 100-ton Brachiosaurus stepped on you?

A: You would be deeply impressed.

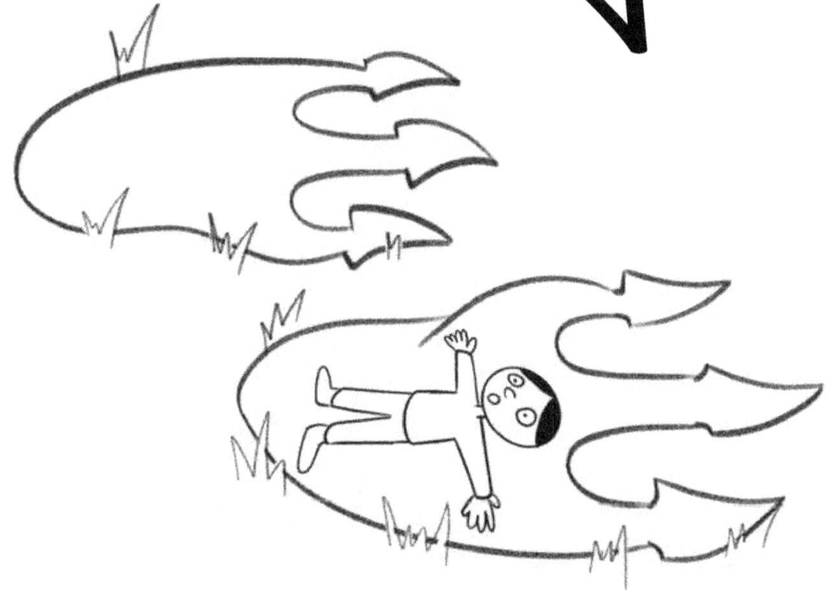

Q: What's a sleeping dinosaur called?

A: Stegosnorus!

Q: What happens if you see a dinosaur in your bed?

A: Go sleep elsewhere!

Q: Do you know what a giant Tyrannosaurus eats?

A: Whatever she wants to!

Q: Never ask a dinosaur to read you a story. You know why?

A: Because their tales are really long.

Q: How can you tell if a dinosaur is under your bed?

A: Your forehead bumps on the ceiling!

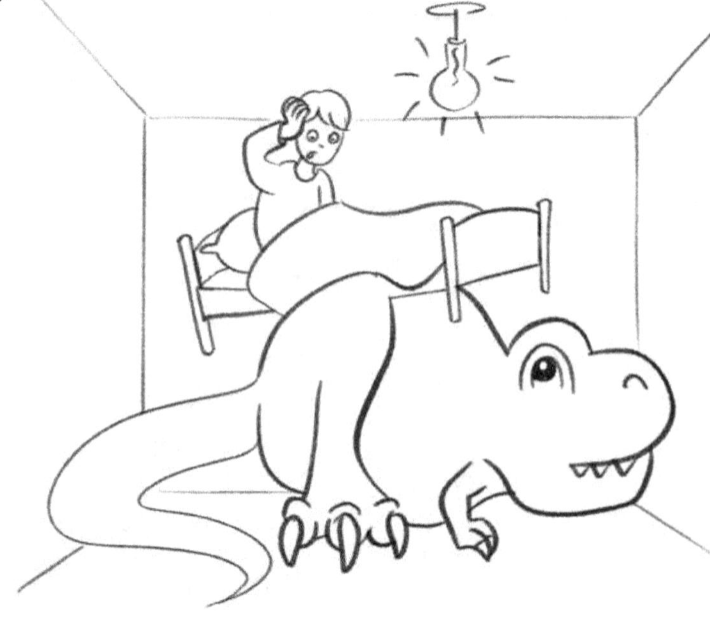

# FOOD
## Jokes

Crack some food jokes, and food lovers will love you.
Here is the list of food jokes to brighten your day:

Q: What's the best thing to put into a pie?

A: Your teeth, of course!

Q: Waiter, do you know why I'm laughing while I eat?

A: Because this food tastes funny!

Q: Did you hear the joke Susan made about peanut butter?

A: Yes, I heard she spread it!

Q: Why do they eat snails in France?

A: Because they don't like fast food!

Q: Why did the fisherman use peanut butter as bait?

A: He wanted to make a jellyfish sandwich!

Q: Who is the father of a baby corn?

A: Pop corn!

Q: Waiter, will my pizza be long?

A: No, sir, it will be round!

Q: What's the name of a rockstar vegetable?

A: Elvis Parsley.

Q: What did my joke do to the egg?

A: It cracked it up!

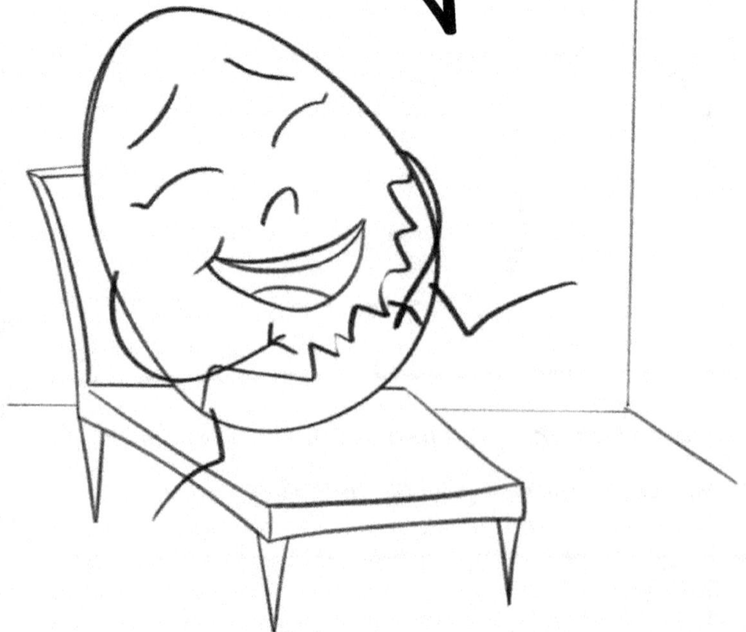

Q: Why is the banana in the hospital?

A: Because it isn't peeling well!

Q: Why can you eat in the desert?

A: All the 'sand which' are there.

Q: Why is the walnut laughing?

A: Because I cracked it up!

Q: What school teaches you how to make ice cream?

A: Sundae School.

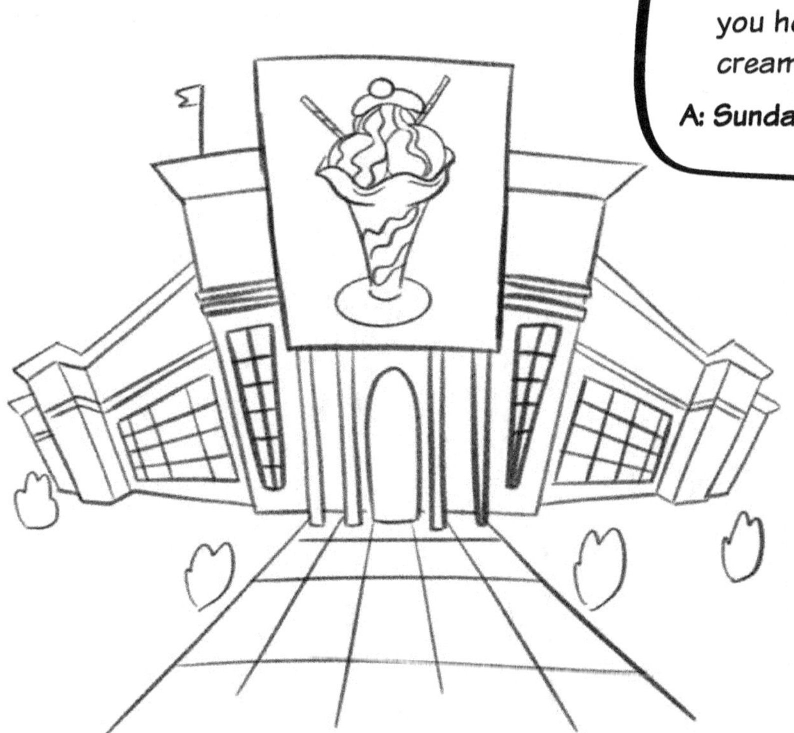

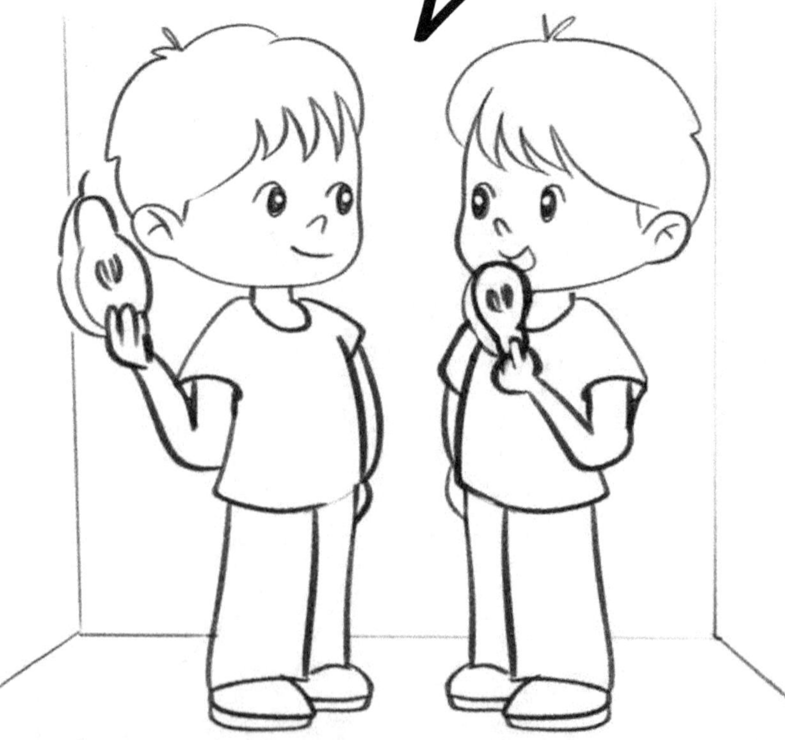
Q: What kind of bread do elves use for sandwiches?
A: Shortbread.
Q: What dance does a pretzel do?
A: The Twist!
Q: If cows make clothes, what does a banana make?
A: Slippers!
Q: What fruit do twins love to eat?
A: Pears!

Q: How do you treat a sick lemon?

A: With lemon aid!

Q: Which peanut went to space?

A: An astronut!

Q: What makes prisoners break out in prison?

A: Chocolate!

Q: Why does the cucumber hate being turned into a pickle?

A: Because it goes through a jarring experience!

Q: When is the only time you GO at red and STOP at green?

A: When you're eating a watermelon!

Q: What will you get if you put three ducks in one box?

A: A box of quackers.

Q: What did the famished computer eat?

A: Chips, one byte at a time.

Q: Why do fish stay clear from the computer?

A: So they don't get hooked on the internet.

Q: Which vegetable broke out of the prison?

A. An *escapea*!

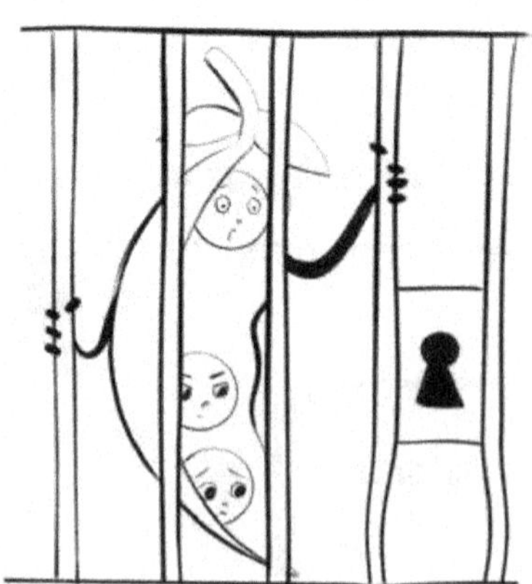

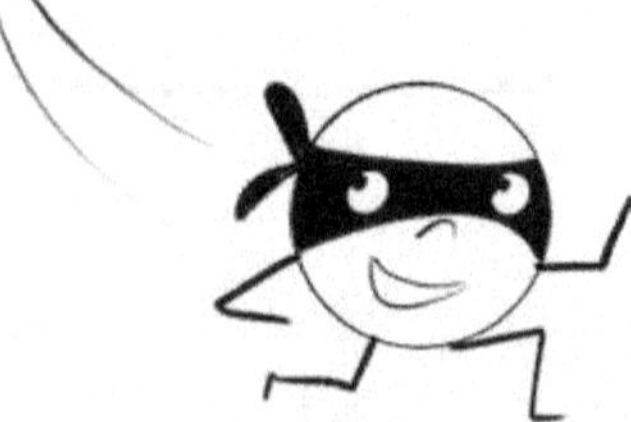

Q: How can you tell whether an elephant has been in your refrigerator?

A: There are footprints in the cheesecake.

Q: What's in an astronaut's favorite sandwich?

A: Launch meat.

Q: What does the mayonnaise say to refrigerator?

A: Close the door, I'm dressing!

Q: Jack: Would you care for some Egyptian Pie?

Jill: What's Egyptian pie?

Jack: The kind mummy used to make.

Q: What starts with "t" ends with "t" and is filled with "t"?

A: A teapot.

Q: Why did the man eat at the bank?

A: He wanted to eat rich food.

Q: What did one knife say to the other?

A: Look sharp!

Q: Why did the man stare at the can of orange juice?

A: Because it said 'concentrate.'

Q: How does the man on the moon eat his food?

A: In satellite dishes.

Q: What's the worst thing about being an octopus?

A: Washing your hands before dinner.

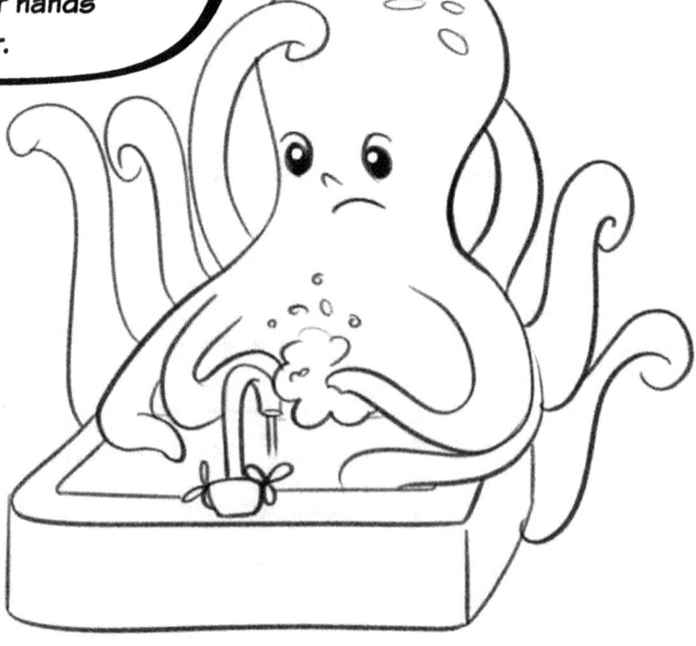

Q: Did you hear the joke about oatmeal?

A: It's a lot of mush.

Q: Why were the pickles embarrassed?

A: They saw the salad dressing!

Q: Did you hear about the fight at the seafood restaurant?

A: Four fish got battered!

Q: Why did the students eat their exam?

A: The teacher said that it was a piece of cake!

Q: When Lee ate raw onions for a week, what did he become?

A: Lone Lee!

Q: What's orange and sounds like a parrot?

A: A carrot.

Q. When potatoes have babies, what are they called?

A: Tater tots.

Q: How do you make an apple turnover?

A: Push it downhill.

Q. What did the pecan say to the walnut?

A: We're friends because we're both nuts.

Q: What's the best way to burn vegetables?

A: Roast them.

Q: Wanna hear a joke about pizza?

A: Never mind, it's too cheesy.

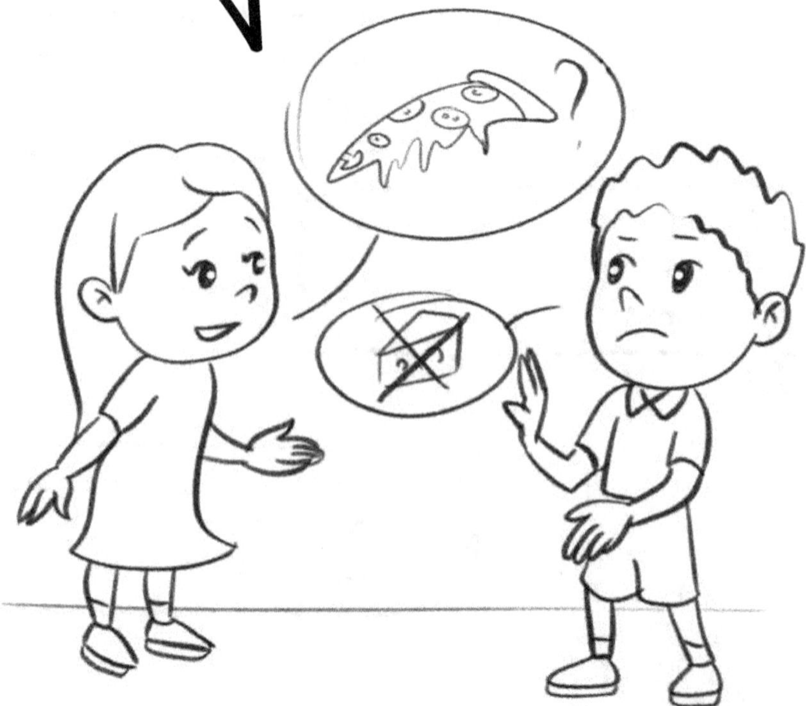

# SPACE
## *Jokes*

**What could be more fascinating and entertaining than the topic of space? Space jokes, that's what!**

Q: Why did Mickey Mouse go to outer space?

A: To find Pluto.

Q: I am throwing a big party in space.

A: Can you help me planet?

Q: Why can't the sun go to college?

A: Because it already has a million degrees!

Q: Where do keyboards go to have dinner?

A: The space bar.

Q: Why can't you teach pupils about space?

A: Because it's too out of this world!

Q: Why did the astronaut break up with her boyfriend?

A: Because she needed some space.

Q: Why couldn't the astronaut put the helmet on his head?

A: Because he didn't have enough space.

Q: Where would an astronaut park his spaceship?

A: A parking meteor.

Q: Why did the people not like the restaurant on the moon?

A: Because there was no atmosphere.

Q: What is an astronaut's favorite chocolate?

A: A Mars bar.

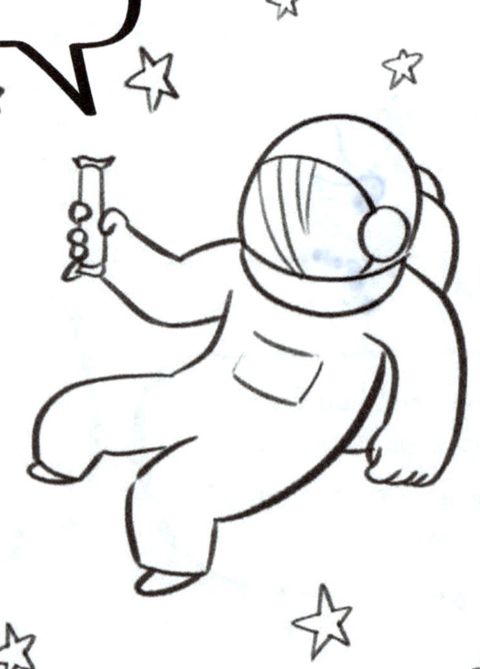

Q: What do you call a comet wrapped in bacon?

A: A meateor.

Q: Why aren't astronauts hungry when they get to space?

A: They had a big launch.

Q: Why did the cow go to outer space?

A: To visit the milky way.

Q: Why did the cow go into the spaceship?

A: It wanted to see the moooooooon.

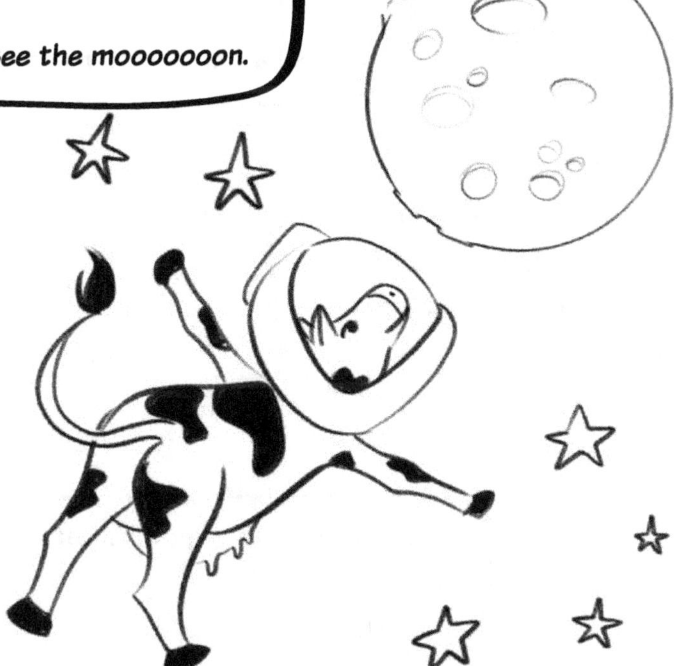

Q: How do you know when the moon has enough to eat?

A: When it's full.

Q: What do planets like to read?

A: Comet books.

Q: Why is Saturn's name the best in our solar system?

A: It has a nice ring to it.

Q: Why did the rocket scientist stop working on a project?

A: He had no comet-ment.

Q: Why haven't aliens come to our solar system yet?

A: They read the reviews: one star.

Q: How does our solar system hold up its pants?

A: With an asteroid belt.

Q: When our solar system was formed, the sun was in charge.

A. So, the planets started a revolution.

Q: I'm reading a book about anti-gravity.

A: It's impossible to put down.

Q: Why didn't the Dog Star laugh at the joke?

A: It was too Sirius.

Q: What should you do if you see a green alien?

A: Wait until it's ripe!

Q: What did the alien say when he was out of room?

A: "I'm all spaced out!"

Q: Why did Venus have to get an air conditioner?

A: Because Mercury moved in.

Q: What did the alien say to the cat?

A: Take me to your litter.

Q: What do you call a loony spaceman?

A: An astronut.

Q: How did the space teddy bear cross the road?

A: Ewoked.

Q: What do you call a lazy man in space?

A: A procrastonaut.

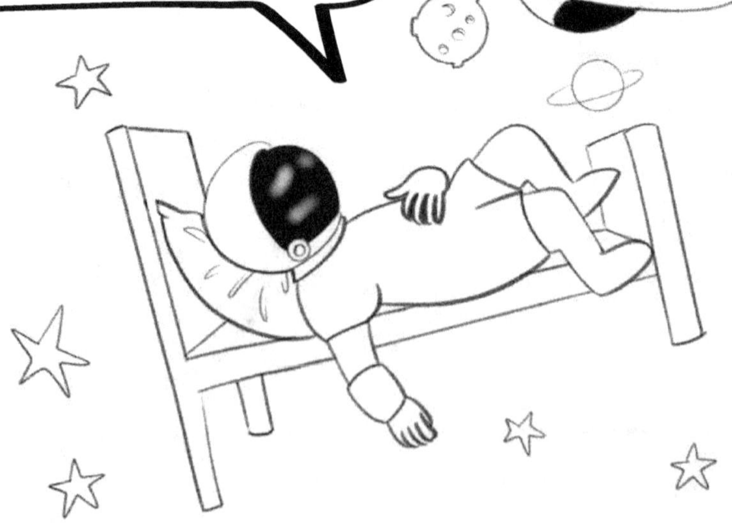

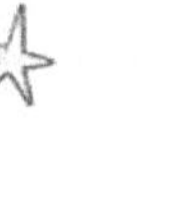

Q: Why will space be a popular tourist spot?

A: The view is breathtaking and will leave you speechless.

Q: If athletes get athlete's foot, then what do astronauts get?

A: Missile-toe.

Q: Who in the solar system has the loosest change?

A: The moon because it keeps changing quarters.

Q: What do you get when you cross a lamb and a rocket?

A: A space sheep!

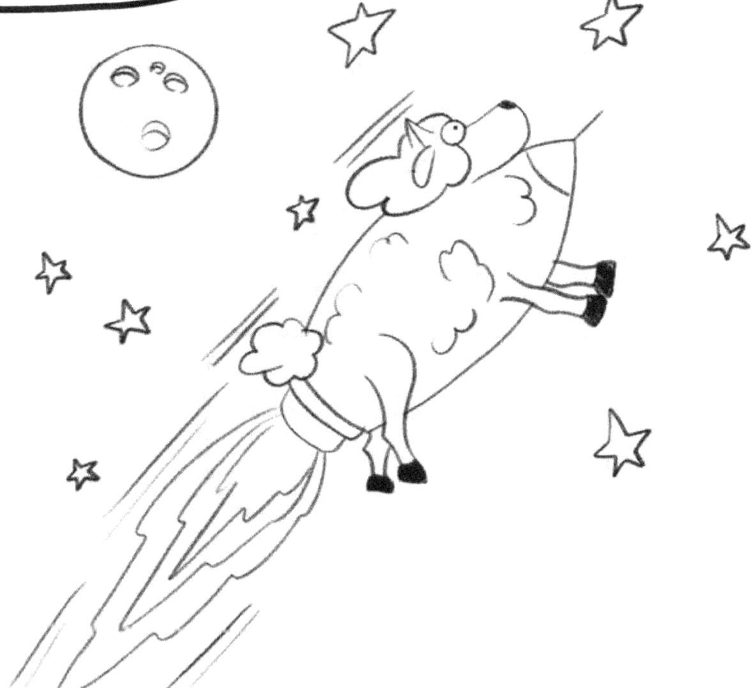

Q: What do you give an alien?

A: Some space!

Q: What school do planets and stars go to, to study?

A: UNIVERSity!

Q: What is fast, loud, and crunchy?

A: A rocket chip!

Q: Why did the alien throw beef on the asteroid?

A: He wanted it a little meteor!

Q: What do you call a tick on the moon?

A: A luna-tick

Q: Why did the rope go to the doctor?

A: There was a knot in its stomach.

Q: Why did Dracula visit the doctor?

A: Because he was coffin!

Q: What happened when Bernard told the doctor about his loss of memory?

A: The doctor made him pay in advance.

Q: Where do you take sick boats to?

A: To the dock!

Q: Why are doctors always calm?

A: They have a lot of patients.

Q: Why did the robot visit the doctor?

A: She had a virus!

Patient: Doctor, I'm dying in 59 seconds!"

Doctor: "Hang on please, I'll be there in a minute."

Patient: Doctor, doctor, I think I'm turning into a curtain.

Doctor: Pull yourself together!

Seven months ago, my doctor told me I was going blind.

I haven't seen him since then.

Q: How did the doctor help the invisible man?

A: He took him to the ICU.

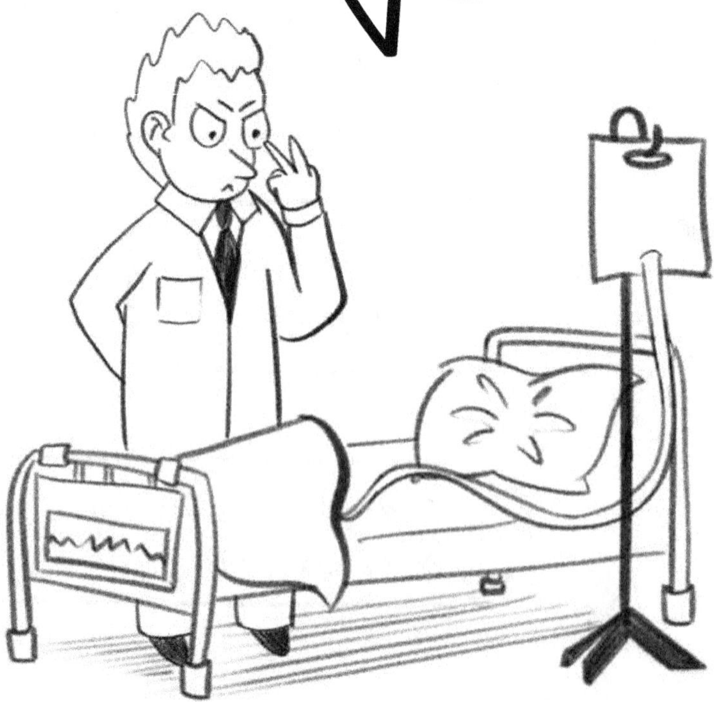

Q: Why was the dermatologist fired?
A: Because he made too many rash decisions.

Q: Why do kings go to the dentist?
A: To get their teeth crowned!

Q: Did you hear the story about the germs?
A: Never mind, I don't want to spread it around.

Q: Why did the cookie go to the hospital?
A: He was feeling crumby.

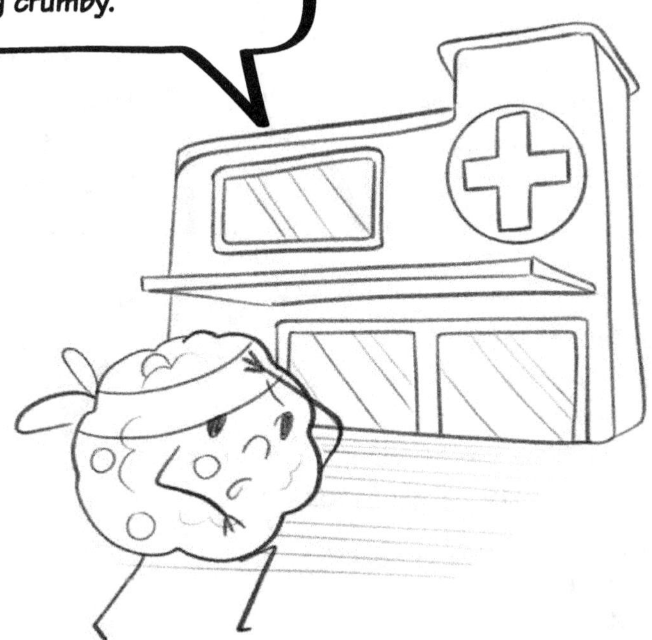

# KNOCK-KNOCK
## Jokes

Knock-knock jokes seem to be a real favorite as they can be made up their own on a daily basis. Below is a list of kid and family-friendly Knock-knock!-jokes to keep your face smiley!

Knock, knock
who's there?
Blame.
Blame who?
Blame yourself.

Knock, knock
who's there?
Mary.
Mary who?
Mary-go-round!

Knock, knock
who's there?
Huhuhu.
Huhuhu who?
Are you an owl?

Knock, knock
who's there?
Ice cream.
Ice cream who?
Ice cream if you waste my time.

Knock, knock
who's there?
Justin.
Justin who?
Just in the knick of time.

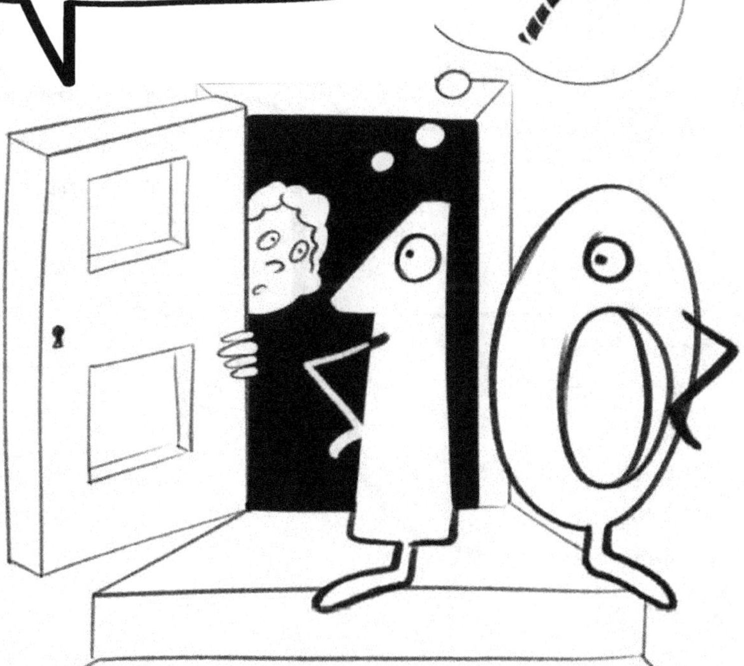
Knock, knock
who's there?
Spell.
Spell who?
W! H! O!

Knock, knock
who's there?
Donut.
Donut who?
Donut open the door.

Knock, knock
who's there?
Tennis.
Tennis who?
Tennis right before eleven.

Knock, knock
who's there?
Lettuce.
Lettuce who?
Lettuce in, please.

Knock, knock
who's there?
Isabelle.
Isabelle who?
Isabelle ringing?

Knock, knock
who's there?
Anita.
Anita who?
Anita another entrance.

Knock, knock
who's there?
Alex.
Alex who?
Alex plain myself later.

Knock, knock
who's there?
Says.
Says who?
Says me.

Knock, knock
who's there?
Hug.
Hug who?
Hug me.

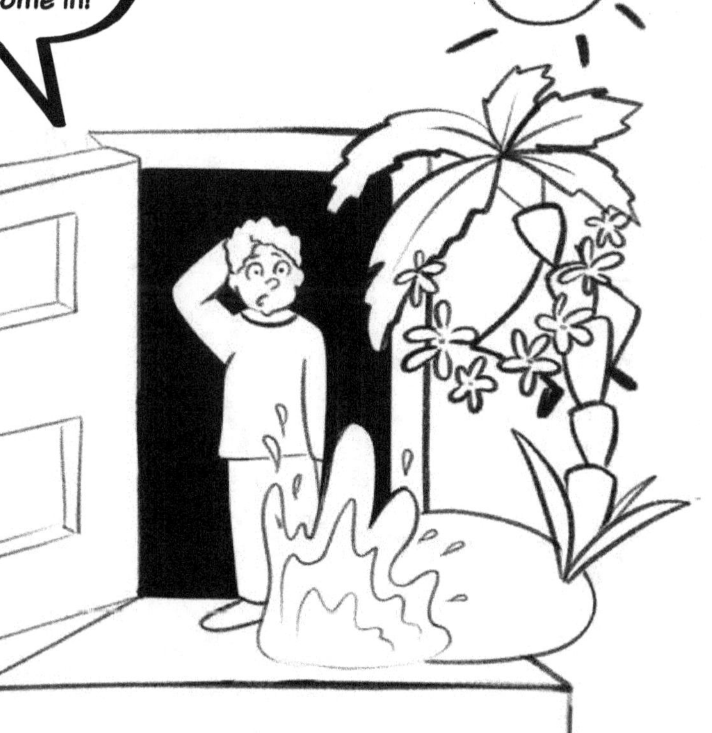
Knock knock
who's there?
Kanu.
Kanu who?
Kan-u open the door?

Knock-knock!
Who's there?
Yul!
Yul who?
Yul see if you open the door!

Knock knock
who's there?
A perfect.
A perfect who?
A perfect visitor.

Knock, knock
who's there?
Hawaii.
Hawaii who?
I'm not fine until I come in!

Knock-knock!
Who's there?
Les!
Les who?
Les party!

Knock Knock!
Who's there?
Omar!
Omar who?
Omar gosh!

Knock Knock!
Who's there?
Organ.
Organ who?
Organ-ize a party in there!

Knock Knock!
Who's there?
Ya!
Ya who?
No, I prefer Gmail!

Knock Knock!
Who's there?
Hippo!
Hippo who?
Hippo birthday to me!

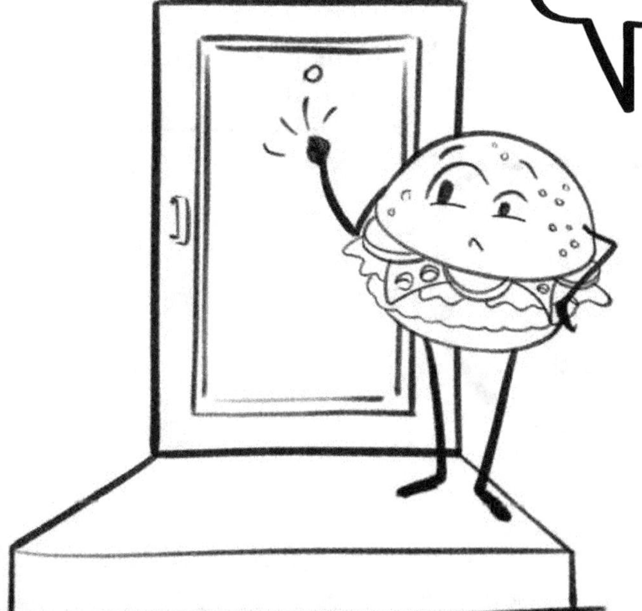

Knock, knock.
Who's there?
Amy.
Amy who?
Amy fraid I can't say my name right now!


Knock, knock.
Who's there?
Barbara.
Barbara who?
Barbara black sheep, have you any wool?


Knock, knock.
Who's there?
Annie.
Annie who?
Annie one in there?


Knock, knock.
Who's there?
Ada.
Ada who?
Ada burger for lunch!

Knock, knock.
Who's there?
Barbie.
Barbie Who?
Barbie Q Chicken!

Knock, knock.
Who's there?
Ben.
Ben who?
Ben here knocking for too long!

Knock, knock.
Who's there?
Candice.
Candice who?
Candice person come in?

Knock, knock.
Who's there?
Doris.
Doris who?
Doris locked, please open for me!

Knock, knock.
Who's there?
Frank.
Frank who?
Frank you for hearing the doorbell.

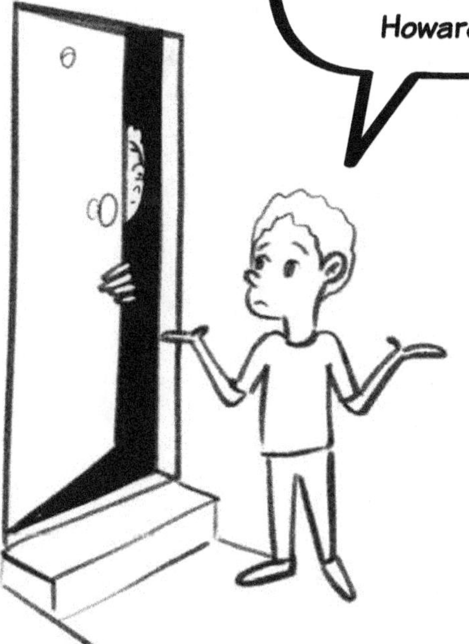

Knock, knock.
Who's there?
Ken.
Ken who?
Ken I come in and spend the night?

Knock, knock.
Who's there?
Lena.
Lena who?
Lena little closer, and I'll tell you!

Knock, knock.
Who's there?
Luke.
Luke who?
Luke at your watch, it's time to party!

Knock, knock.
Who's there?
Howard.
Howard who?
Howard I know?

Knock, knock.
Who's there?
Nana.
Nana who?
Nana your business who I am.

Knock, knock.
Who's there?
Otto.
Otto who?
Otto know what you are doing in there!

Knock, knock.
Who's there?
Wendy.
Wendy who?
Wendy door's opened, I'll tell you who I am.

Knock, knock.
Who's there?
Nobel.
Nobel who?
No bell, please get one!

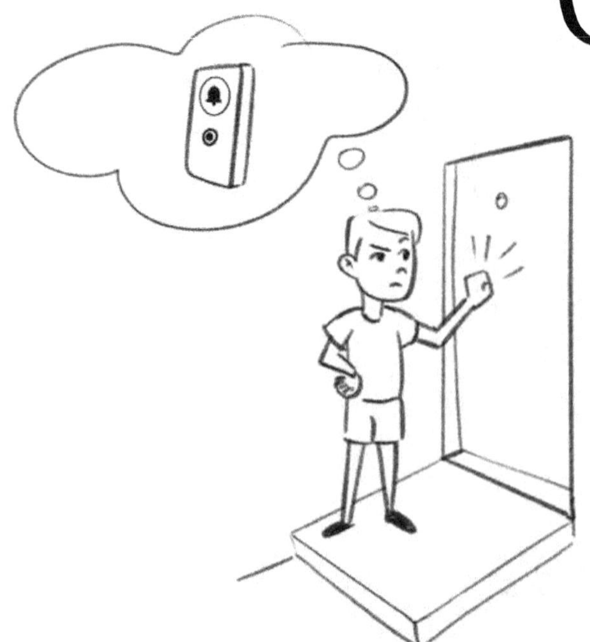

Knock, knock.
Who's there?
Will.
Will who?
Will you let me in or not?

Knock, knock.
Who's there?
Oslo.
Oslo who?
Oslo down; it's the billionaire!

Knock, knock.
Who's there?
Howl.
Howl who?
Howl you know who it is unless you open the door?

Knock, knock.
Who's there?
Leash.
Leash who?
Leash you could do is open the door.

Knock, knock.
Who's there?
Butter.
Butter who?
Butter be quick; I have to go to the restroom!

Knock, knock.
Who's there?
Scold.
Scold who?
Scold out here, please let me in!

Knock, knock.
Who's there?
Figs.
Figs who?
Figs the doorbell, it's not working well!

Knock, knock.
Who's there?
Ketchup.
Ketchup who?
Ketchup with my time, please!

Knock, knock.
Who's there?
Europe.
Europe who?
No, I'm not!

Knock, knock.
Who's there?
Amarillo.
Amarillo who?
Amarillo great guy.

Knock, knock.
Who's there?
Police.
Police who?
Police open the door, it's freezing out here!

Knock, knock.
Who's there?
Cher.
Cher who?
Cher would like it if you let me in!

Knock, knock.
Who's there?
Theodore.
Theodore who?
Won't you open Theodore already?

Knock, knock.
Who's there?
Stopwatch.
Stopwatch who?
Stopwatch your doing and open up the door!

Knock, knock.
Who's there?
Robin.
Robin who?
Robin you, stick 'em up!

Knock, knock.
Who's there?
Icy.
Icy who?
Icy you standing there, open the door already!

Knock, knock.
Who's there?
Voodoo.
Voodoo who?
Voodoo you think? It's me.

Knock, knock.
Who's there?
Iva.
Iva who?
Iva sore hand from all this knocking!

Knock, knock.
Who's there?
Canoe.
Canoe who?
Canoe please let me in?

Knock, knock.
Who's there?
Needle.
Needle who?
Needle little help getting inside, please.

Knock, knock.
Who's there?
Mustache.
Mustache who?
Open up, I mustache you a question.

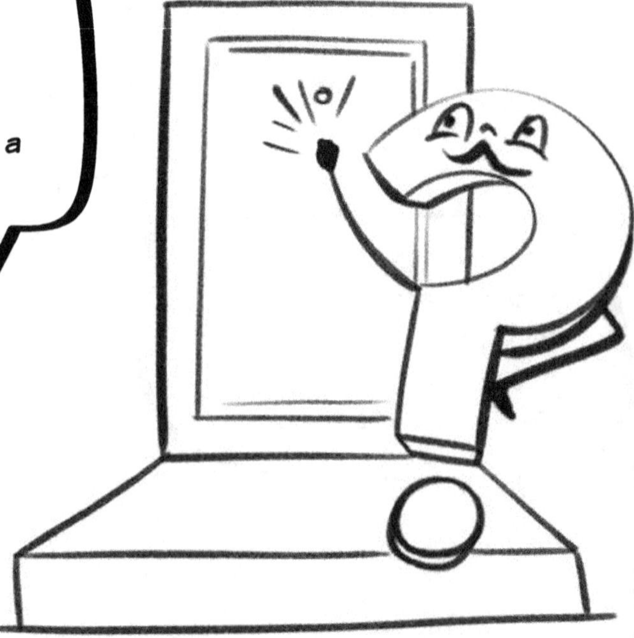

Knock, knock.
Who's there?
Watson.
Watson who?
Watson TV right now?



Knock, knock.
Who's there?
Dishes.
Dishes who?
Dishes is a really nice place!



Knock, knock.
Who's there?
Anee.
Anee who?
Anee one you want!



Knock, knock.
Who's there?
A herd.
A herd who?
A herd you were home, so I thought I'd stop by.



Knock, knock.
Who's there?
Avenue.
Avenue who?
Avenue heard me knock before?

Knock, knock.
Who's there?
Ivor.
Ivor who?
Ivor got!

Knock, knock.
Who's there?
Viper.
Viper who?
Viper nose, it's running!

Knock, knock.
Who's there?
Norma Lee.
Norma Lee who?
Norma Lee it doesn't take this long
for someone to open the door!

Knock, knock.
Who's there?
Roach.
Roach who?
Roach you a letter, did you get it?

Knock, knock.
Who's there?
Claire.
Claire who?
Claire a path, I'm coming in!

Knock, knock.
Who's there?
Summer D.
Summer D who?
Summer D who wants you
to open the door.

Knock, knock.
Who's there?
Harry.
Harry who?
Harry up and let me in already.

Knock, knock.
Who's there?
Hatch.
Hatch who?
Bless you!

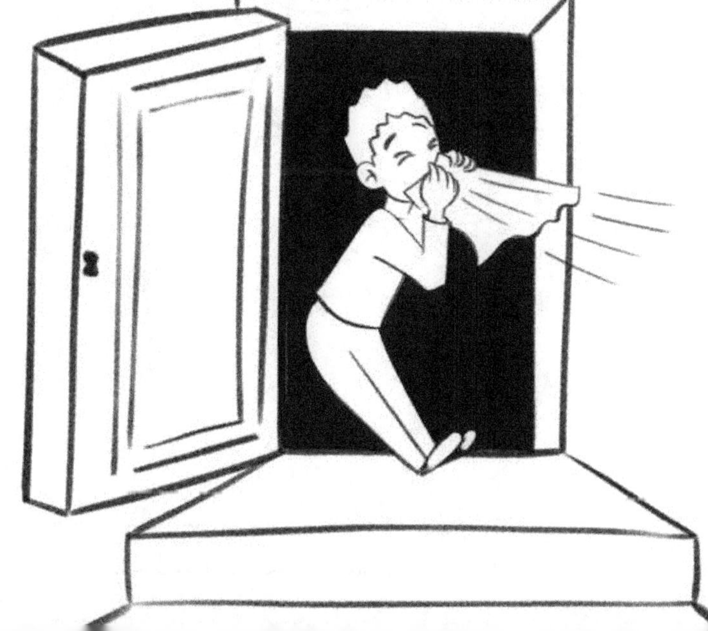

# CORNY
## Jokes

Good corny jokes turn a bad day into a good one.
They are funny and sometimes a bit  stupid but actually make sense to the
intelligent! These jokes are so bad but so good to jokesters.

Q: What's the most important
thing to put into cheese?

A: Your teeth!

Q:  Why do cars always
go on the road?

A: Because it's impossible
to go on the air.

Q: Why was the mathematics
teacher sad?

A: Because he had too many
problems to solve.

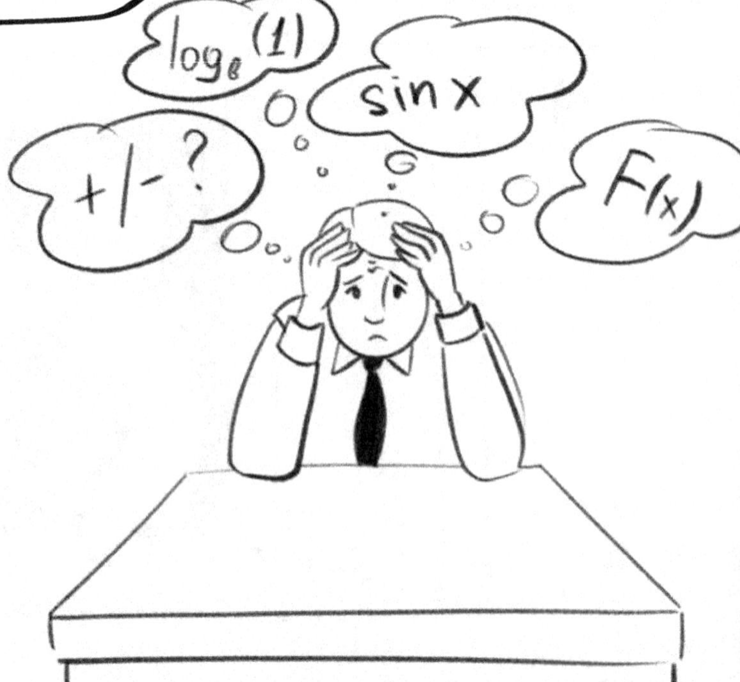

Q: Where was the kid going with the ladder?

A: To high school.

Q: What did the hammer do when it got angry?

A: Hit the nail on the head.

Q: What did the roasted chicken say to the dog?

A: Nothing. Roasted chickens can't talk.

Q: What do you call a donkey without an eye?

A: A Donk.

Q: Why can't my dogs be good dancers?

A: Because they have two left feet.

Q: What do you get when you cross an elephant with a fish?

A: Swimming trunks.

Q: What did number zero say to number eight?

A: Nice belt!

Q. Why are robots never afraid?

A: They have nerves made of steel.

Q: Why did Nelly throw the clock out of the window?

A: He wanted to see time fly.

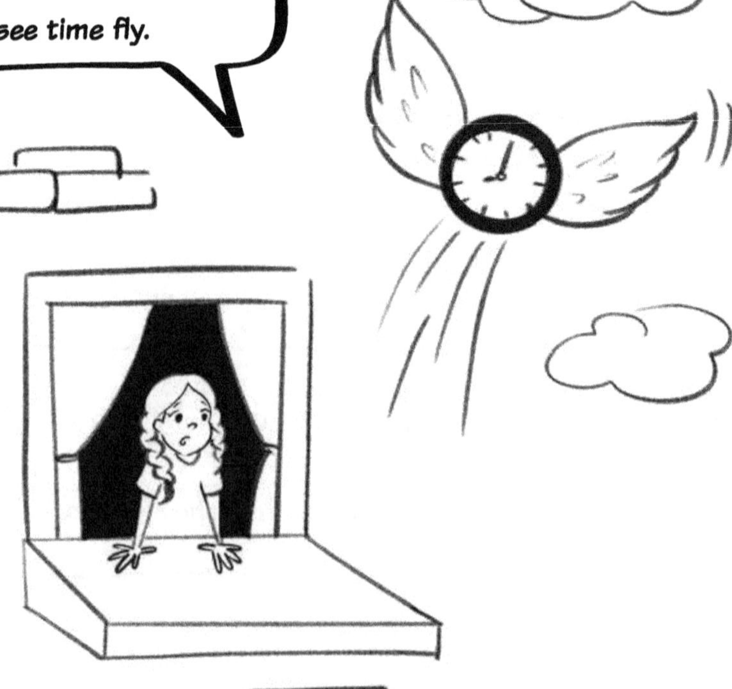

Q: Why couldn't the pirate play cards?

A: He was sitting on the deck!

Q: What's the difference between a TV and a newspaper?

A: Ever tried hitting a fly with a TV?

Q: Why was the boy's belt arrested?

A: Because it held up some pants!

Q: What do you get when you cross a turtle with a parrot?

A: A walkie-talkie.

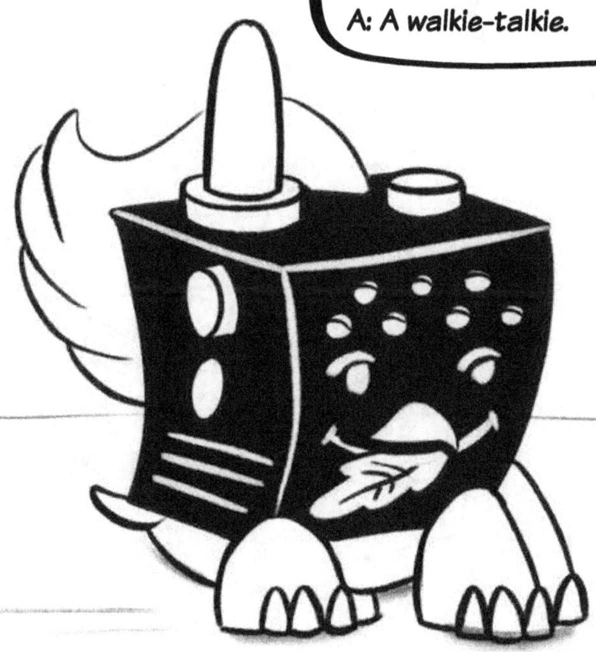

Q: Why was everyone so exhausted on April the 1st?

A: They had just finished Marching for 31 days.

Q: Why do we have to go to bed every night?

A: Because the bed won't come to us!

Q: Why did Jacob go out with a prune?

A: Because he couldn't find a date!

Q: What has four wheels and flies?

A: A garbage truck!

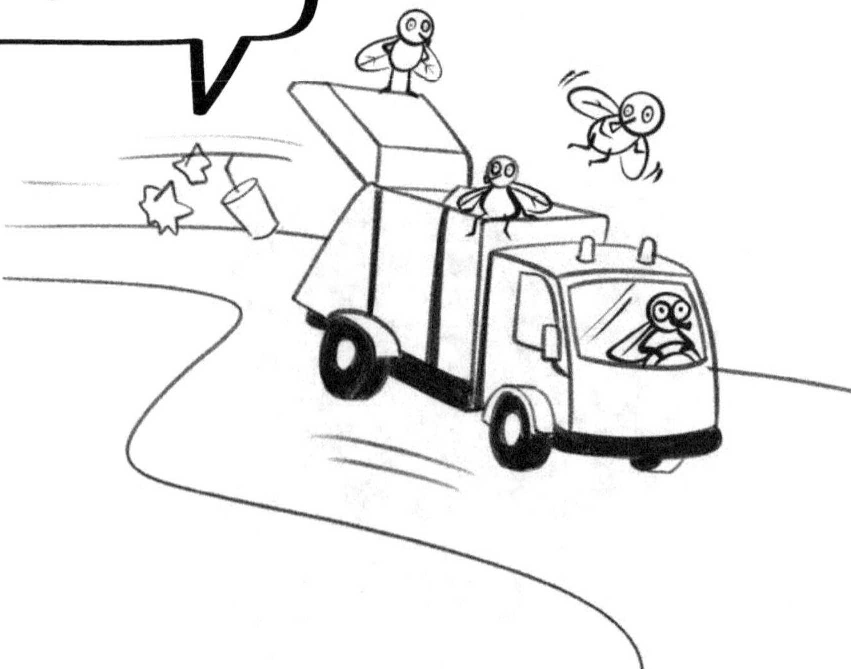

Q: Why do Eskimos do their laundry in the tide?

A: Because it's too cold out-tide!

Q: What kind of car does Mickey Mouse's wife cruise in?

A: A Minnie van!

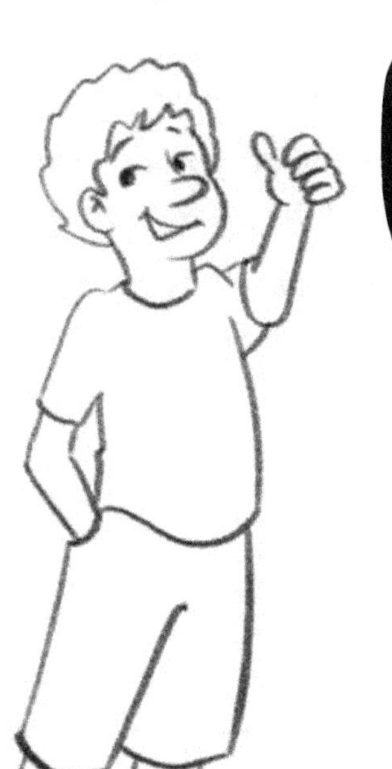

Q: What do you call a shoe made out of banana peels?

A: Slippers.

Q: What fish do knights like to eat?

A: Swordfish.

Q: What do you call a laptop that sings?

A: A Dell.

Q: Why do watermelons have weddings?

A: Because they cantaloupe.

Q: What do you call it when you get hit by a bike every day?

A: A vicious cycle.

Q: What did the sink say to the toilet?

A: You look flushed!

Q: Why won't the crab share his treasure?

A: He's shellfish.

30. Q: Why did the bicycle fall over?

A: It was two tired.

Q: Why did the guy climb the ladder?

A: To get to the top.

Q: Why should golfers always bring extra pants?

A: In case they get a hole in one.

Q: Did you hear? There was a kidnapping at school.

A: Don't worry, he woke up.

Q: What do you call a pig that knows kung-fu?

A: Pork chop.

Q: Wanna know why I sold my
   vacuum?

A: All it did was collect dust.

Q: Do you know why Waldo wears stripes?

A: He doesn't want to be spotted.

Q: Why won't vampires drink from
   Taylor Swift?

A: She's got bad blood.

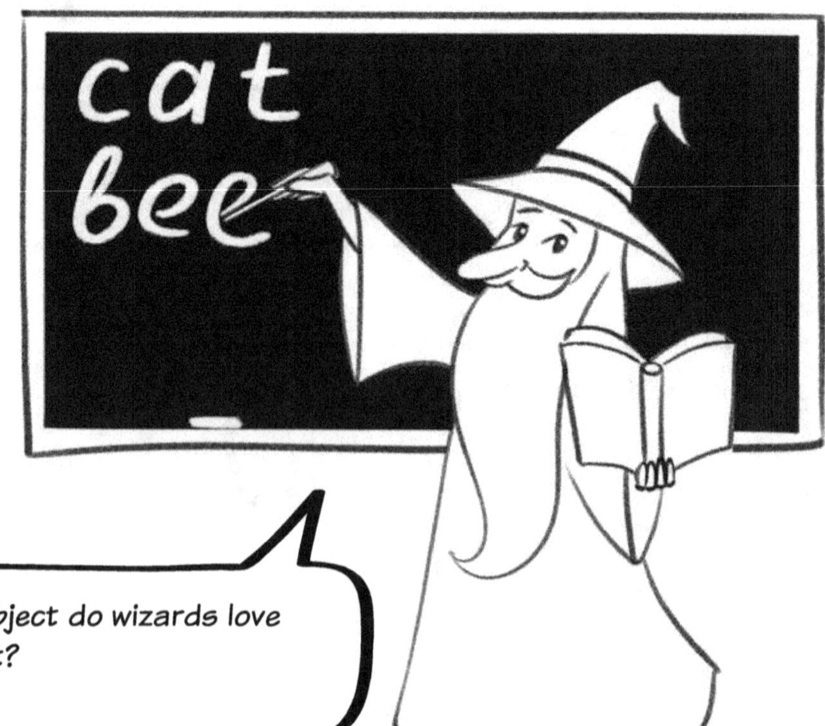


Q: What subject do wizards love
   the most?

A: Spelling.

Q: What did the scarf say to the hat?

A: You go on ahead, I'll hang around.

Q: What did the one eye say to the other?

A: Just between you and me, something smells.

Q: Have you read the book about zero-gravity?

A: It's impossible to put down.

Q: What do you call a clever duck?

A: A wise quacker.

Q: What do you call someone who sees an Apple store get robbed?

A: An iWitness.

Q: What do spies do when it's cold?

A: They go undercover.

Q: Why can't a hand be 12 inches long?

A: Because then it would be a foot.

Q: What's Forrest Gump's password?

A: 1Forrest1.

Q: What does the moon do to cut its hair?

A: Eclipse it.

# CROSS
## the road

'Why did the chicken cross the road?' is a popular kind of joke, so classic and hilarious and we never seem to tire of them. It starts with a simple question, though some kids and jokesters have now taken it further. It's not only about chickens, you know; we also wish to know why other animals cross the road. Enjoy the list.

Q: Why did the white rooster cross the road?

A: Because he wasn't chicken.

Q: Why did the baby chick cross the road?

A: It was take-your-child-to-work day.

Q: Why did the gum cross the road?

A: It was stuck to the chicken's foot.

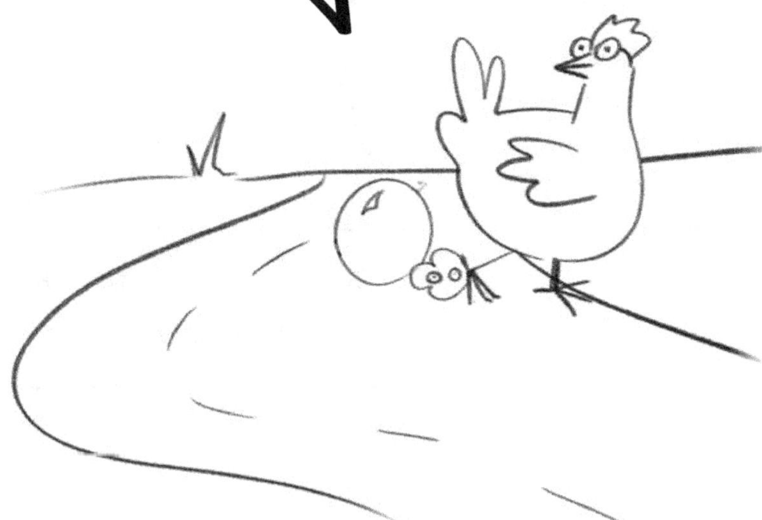

Q: Why did the potato run across the road?

A: So it wouldn't get mashed.

Q: Why was everyone mad at the pig crossing the road?

A: Because he was a road hog.

Q: Why didn't the skeleton cross the road?

A: Because he didn't have the guts.

Q: Why did the chicken family cross the road?

A: They thought it was an egg-cellent idea.

Q: Why did the dinosaur cross the road?

A: The chicken wasn't around yet.

Q: Why did the fish cross the ocean?

A: To get to the other tide.

A: Why did the spider cross the road?

A: To get to his website.

Q: Why did the fish cross the road?

A: To get to its school.

Q: Why did the cow cross the road?

A: To get to the udder side.

Q: Why did the pillow cross the road?

A: It was picking up the chicken's feathers.

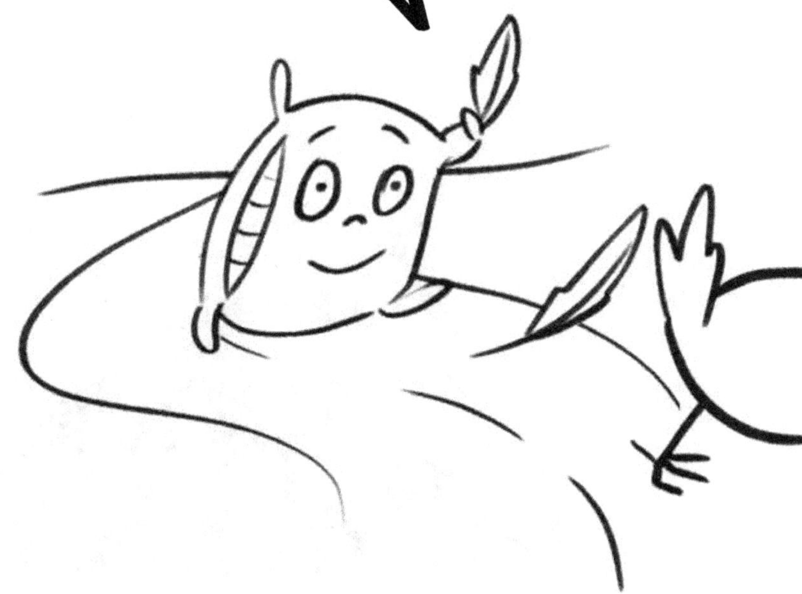

Q: Why did the cow cross the road?

A: So he could go to the MOO-vies.

Q: Why did the duck cross the road?

A: To prove he's no chicken.

Q: Why did the chicken cross the road?

A: To avoid this lame and outdated joke.

Q: Why did the raccoon cross the road?

A: He saw you put out the garbage for pickup.

Q: Why did the zebra cross the road?

A: Because it was a zebra crossing.

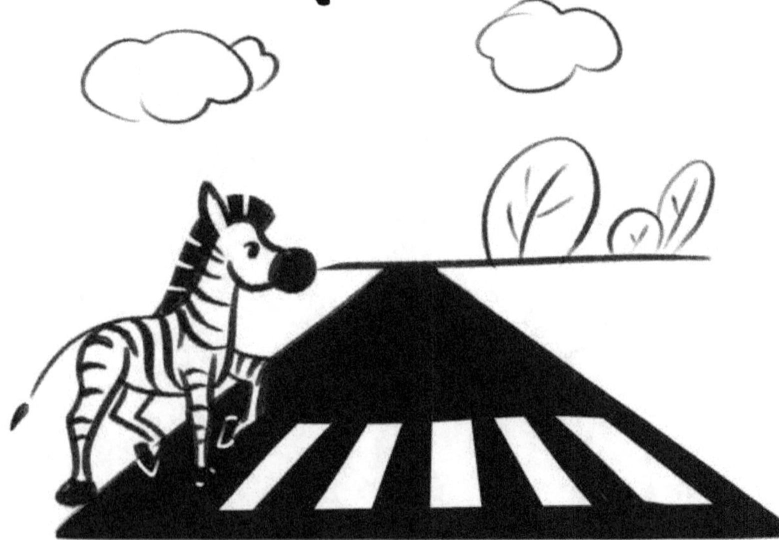

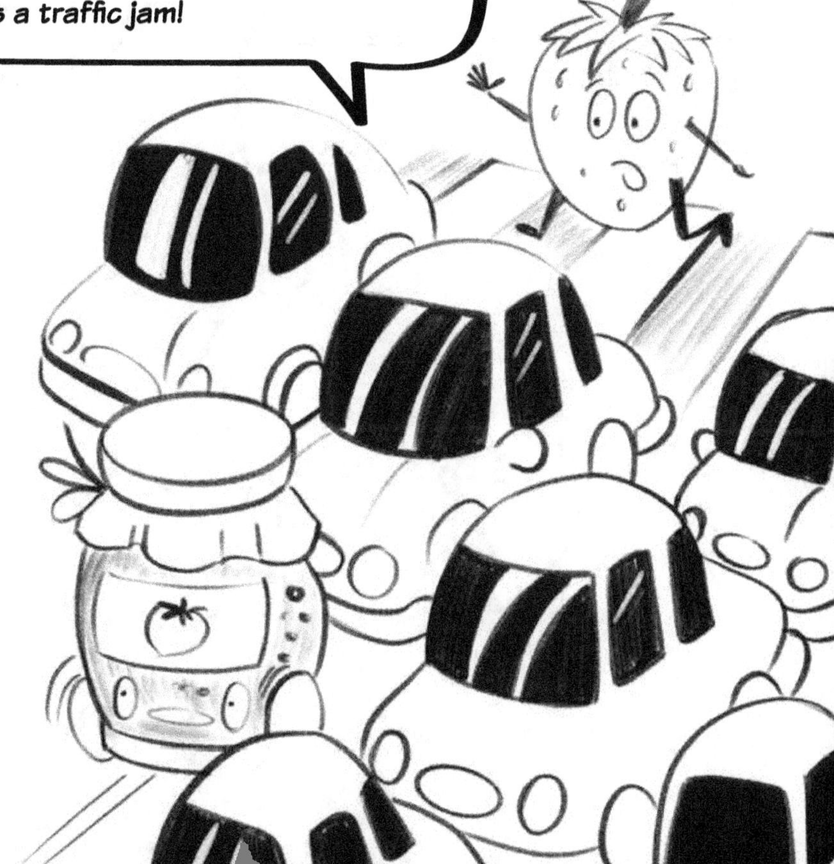
Q: How did the sushi cross the road?
A: He was rolling.
Q: Why did the PowerPoint presentation cross the road?
A: To get to the other slide.
Q: Why did the turkey cross the road?
A: It was Thanksgiving Day, and it wanted people to think it was a chicken!
Q: Why did the strawberry cross the road?
A: There was a traffic jam!

# MUSIC
## Jokes

You just can't live without music, and what better way to appreciate those sweet sounds than to make a joke of them? Here are some sharp musical jokes that are sure to make you the comedic maestro of the playground.

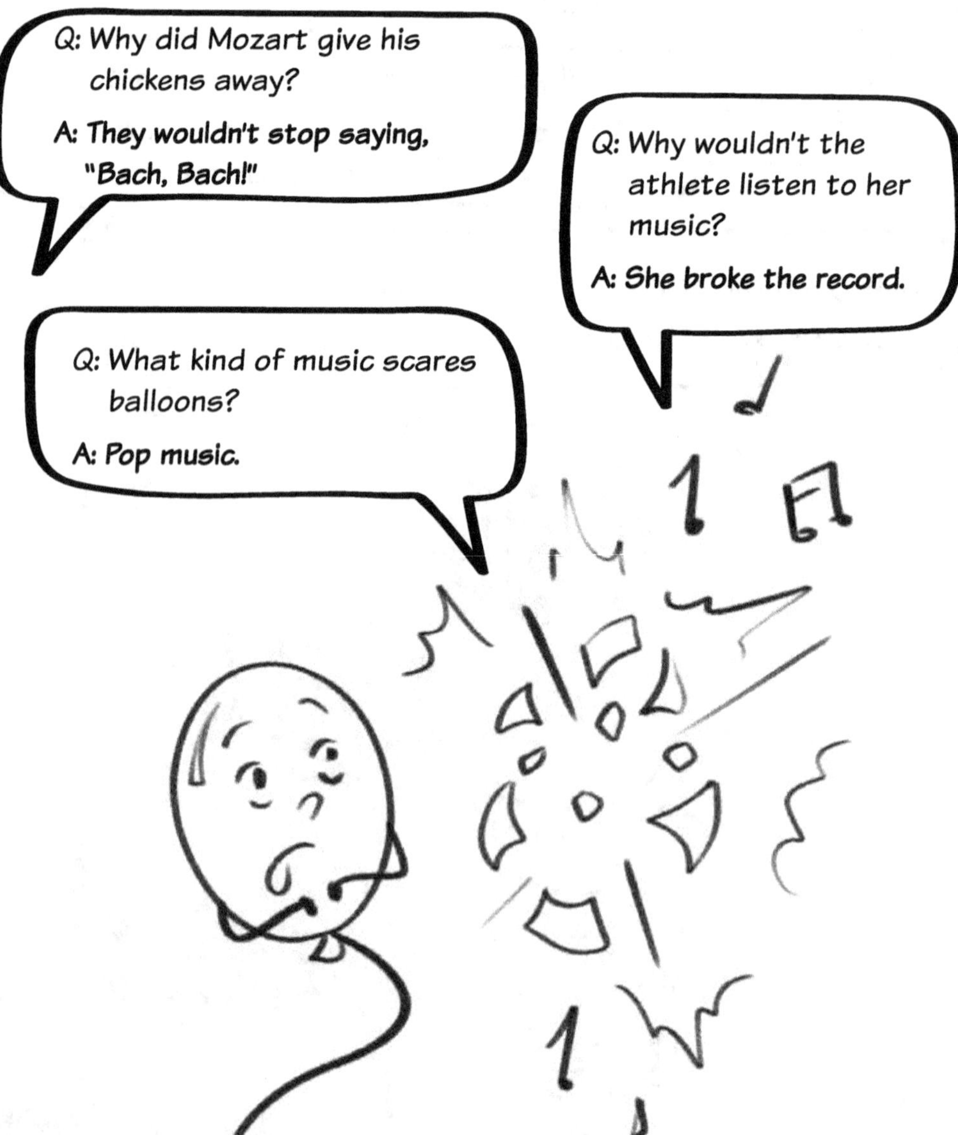

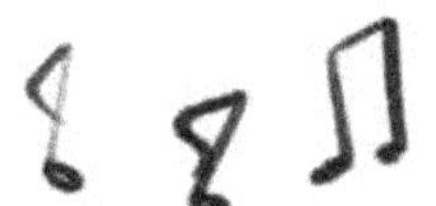

Q: What makes music on your head?

A: Headbands.

Q: What's the most musical part of a chicken?

A: The drumstick.

Q: What's the difference between a piano and a fish?

A: You can't tuna fish.

Q: Why did the boy climb the ladder to sing?

A: So he could reach the high notes.

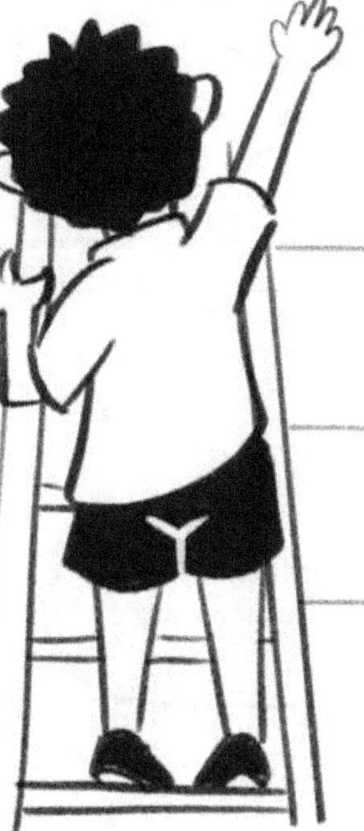

Q: What sings and has thirty feet?

A: A choir.

Q: What's the most musical part of a snake?

A: Its scales.

Q: Where did the musician leave his keys?

A: At the piano.

Q: What do you call a cow that plays an instrument?

A: Moo-sician.

Q: Why are pirates so good at singing?

A: They can hit the high Cs!

# SCHOOL
## *Jokes*

A lot of funny things happen in school which could keep us entertained for a long time! Most of these jokes are the things people imagine in their thoughts concerning school and education. Ready tolaugh?

Q: What did the floor say to the earthquake?

A: Do not crack me up!

Q: What is the worst thing you'll most likely find in a school cafeteria?

A: The food.

Q: What did the pencil ask the pen?

A: What is your point?

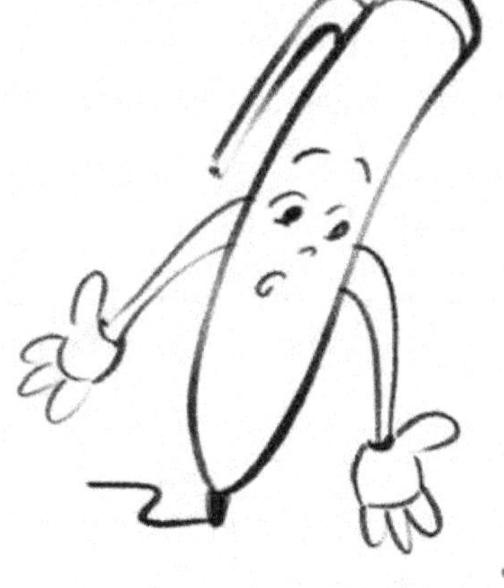
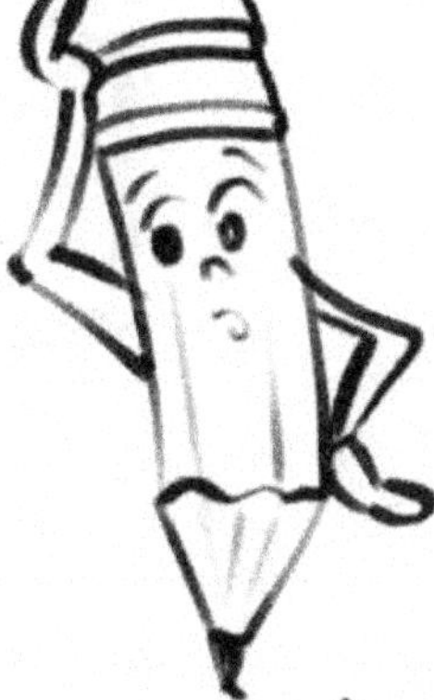

Q: Why did the nose avoid going to school?

A: He did not want to get picked on!

Q: How does one get straight A's?

A: By making use of a ruler.

Q: Why was the child studying on the airplane?

A: So he can get a higher education!

Q: Why did the music instructor getf locked in the classroom?

A: Because the keys were in the piano!

Q: What do elves study in their school?

A: The elf-abet!

Q: What's the world's largest building?

A: The library because it has many 'stories'.

Q: What vegetables do librarians prefer?

A: Quiet peas.

Q: Why did the new student steal a chair?

A: Because the teacher told him to take a seat.

Q: Which tools does one need for math?

A: Multi-PLIERS.

Q: Why did the jellybean attend school?

A: So it could become a smartie!

Q: Why did the school teacher visit the beach?

A: So he could test the water.

Q: What does a thesaurus have for breakfast?

A: A synonym roll.

Q: Why did the broom arrive late for school?

A: He over swept.

Q: What did one calculator say to the other?

A: Count on me.

Q: Can you do a math test in the jungle?

A: No, because there are many cheetahs!

Q: What does one call a square that is involved in an accident?

A: A WRECKtangle.

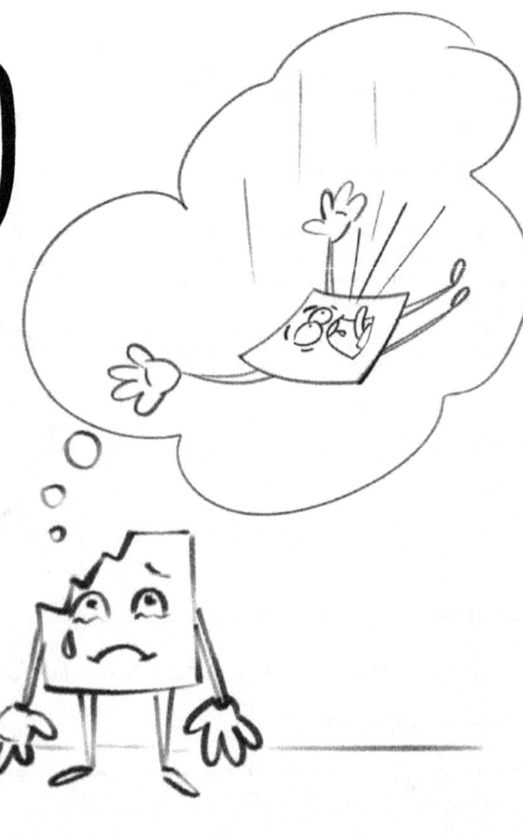

Q: Where's the best place to grow flowers?

A: In a kinderGARDEN.

Q: What is gray on the inside and yellow on the outside?

A: A school bus filled with elephants.

Q: What kind of bet cannot be won?

A: An Alphabet.

Q: What did one maths book say to the other?

A: "I have lots of problems."

Q: How did the student drown?

A: Because his grades were below C-level!

Q: Where did the pencil spend its vacation?

A: In Pennsylvania.

Q: Why is the voice instructor so great at baseball?

A: Because he has the perfect pitch.

Q: What does one get when you cross a teacher and a tiger?

A: I do not know, but you better behave in class!

Q: How do New York City Children learn their multiplication tables?

A: In Times Square.

Q: What kind of math do owls solve?

A: Owlgebra.

Q: Why did the triangle and square visit the gym?

A: In order to stay in shape!

Q: Why was the pencil first to cross the road?

A: Because he was the LEADer!

Q: What is the worst that could happen to a geography teacher?

A: Getting lost.

Q: How do ducks solve math?

A: Using a QUACK-ulator!

Q: What does the cross-eyed teacher say to the principal?

A: "I cannot control my pupils!"

Q: What did the student say to the math problem?

A: Solve your problems; I am not your therapist!

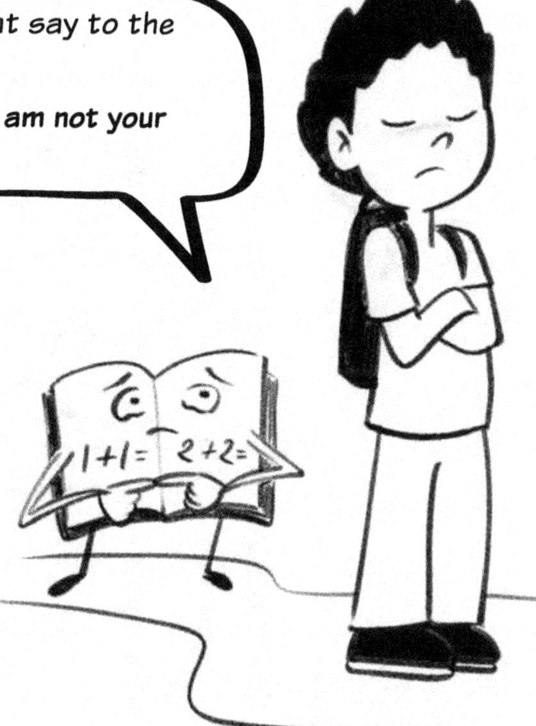

Q: What lurks around the kindergarten at night?

A: An alpha-BAT.

Q: What did the ghost teacher tell its class?

A: "Look at the board, or I will go through it again!"

Q: What does one call a boy with a dictionary in his pockets?

A: Smarty Pants!

Q: Why did 6 eat 7?

A: Because 7 8 9.

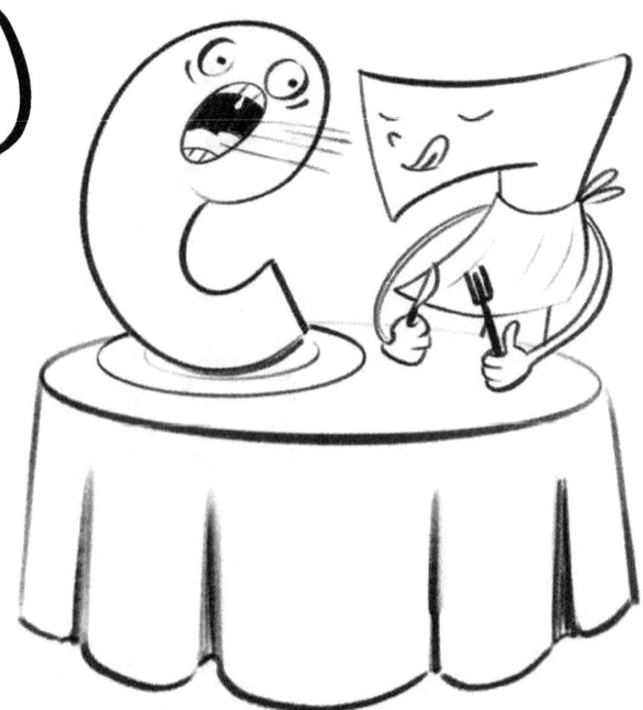

Q: Why did the teacher write on the window?

A: Because he wanted to make the lesson very clear!

Q: Why did the teacher put on sunglasses?

A: Because all his students were so bright!

Q: What did the snake study in school?

A: Hiss tory.

Knock Knock!
**Who is there?**
Dewey.
**Dewey who?**
Dewey have to attend school today?

Teacher: I see you missed the first day of school.

Kid: Yes, but I did not miss it very much.

# BIRTHDAY
## Jokes

Throw any of these birthday jokes to family members, and they'll catch it with pleasure. Everyone wishes to be happy and loved, especially on their birthdays. You can choose to write any of these questions on a piece of paper to the birthday boy of girl,watch the reaction on his face, and you'll love it. Then ask for his reply or answer. Enjoy the jokes!

Q: Why do candles always go on top of cakes?

A: It's difficult to light them from the bottom.

Q: What goes up but never comes down?

A: Your age.

Q: What do you say to a kangaroo on its birthday?

A: Hoppy Birthday!

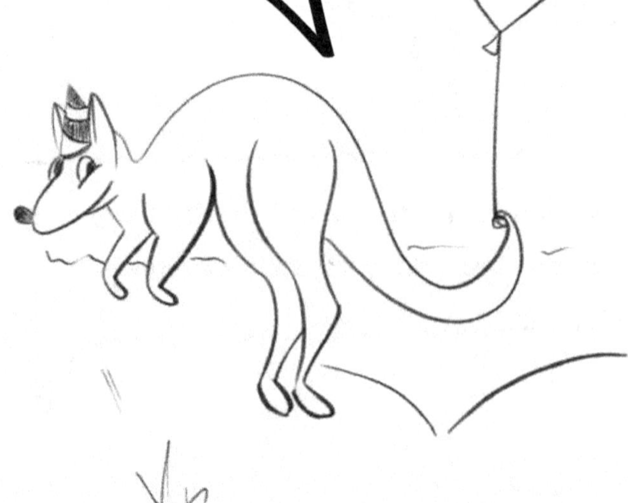

Q: What did the pirate say on his 80th birthday?

A: Aye matey.

Q: What did the tiger say to her cub on his birthday?

A: It's roar birthday!

Q: Why did the girl put her cake in the freezer?

A: She wanted to ice it.

Q: What do you give a 3100 pound. rhino for his birthday?

A: I don't know, but you better hope he likes it.

Q: Why did the robber break into the bakery?

A: She heard the cakes were rich.

Q: What did the cake say to the ice cream?

A: You're cool.

Q: How do pickles celebrate their birthday?

A: They relish it.

Q: What's the cleanest type of birthday party joke?

A: One that's a soap-prise.

Q: What do clams like to do on their birthdays?

A: Shell-ebrate.

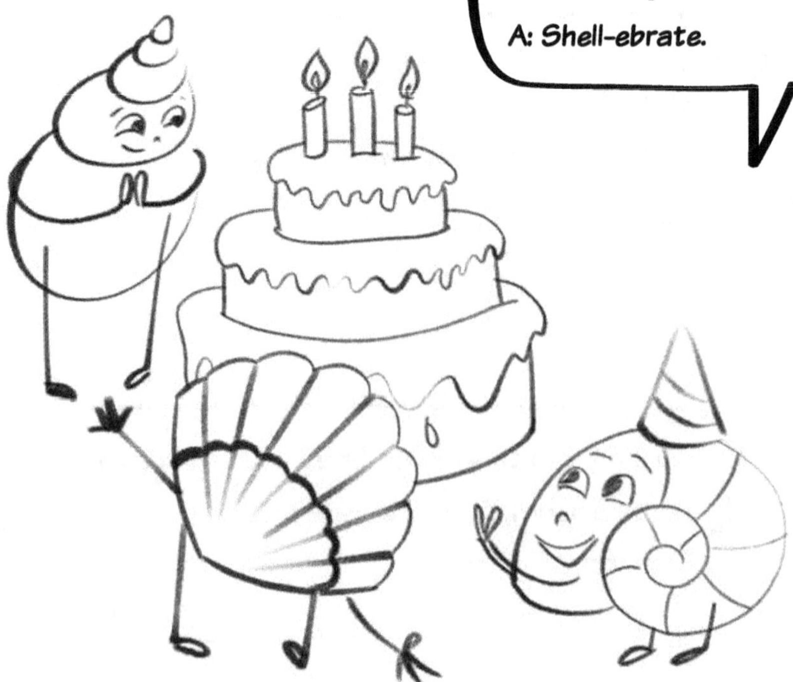

Q: Why can't kids remember their infant birthdays?

A: Because they are too focused on the present.

Q: What did one candle say to the other?

A: Don't birthdays just burn you out?

Q: Why was the birthday cake so hard?

A: It was a marble cake!

Knock knock!
**Who's there?**
Wanda.
**Wanda who?**
Wanda wish you a happy birthday, friend!

Q: What happens when your dad chugs eight sodas at your birthday party?

A: He burps 7-Up.

Q: What do frogs drink at their birthday parties?

A: Diet croak.

Q: How do cats bake a cake?

A: From scratch!

Q: What happens if no one comes to your birthday party?

A: You can have your cake and eat it, too.

Teacher: Tom, why are you crying?
Tom: Because it's my birthday.
Teacher: You should be happy on your birthday.
Tom: Babies cry when they come out of the womb.

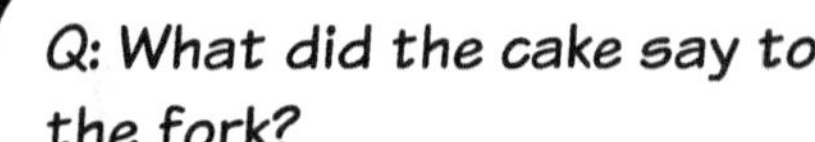

Q: What did the cake say to the fork?

A: You wanna piece of me?

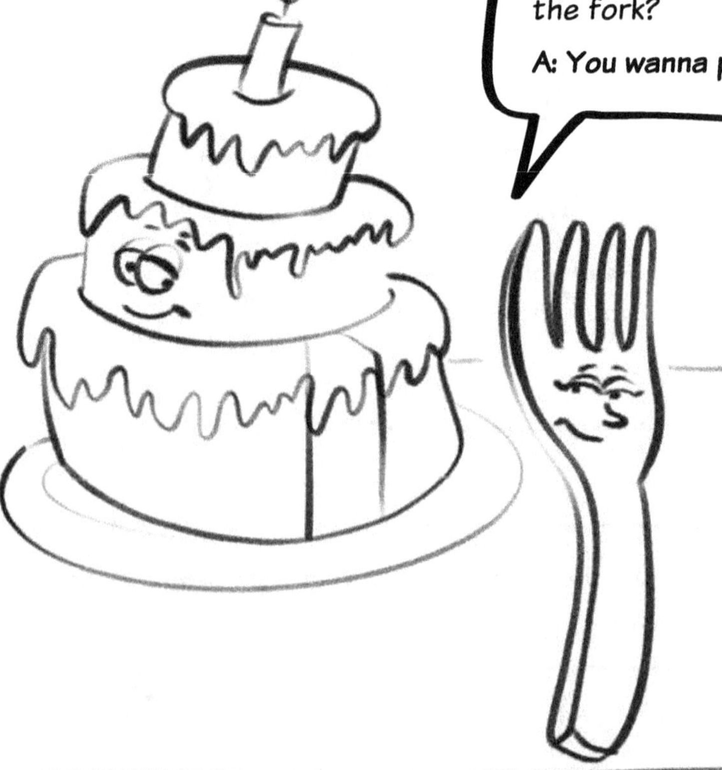

Q: Why did the cupcake cross the road?

A: It had muffin else to do!

Q: Why don't owls give each other presents on their birthdays?

A: Because they don't give a hoot!

Q: What did the mama say to her baby on his birthday?

A: Nappy Birthday!

Q: What did one plate say to the other plate?

A: "Dinner's on me!"

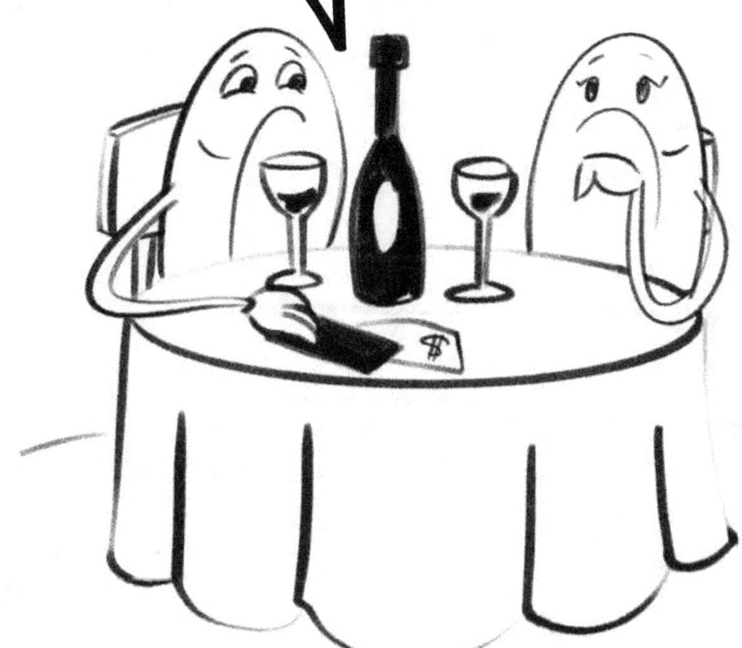

Q: What is it about birthdays that make kangaroos unhappy?

A: They only get to celebrate them in leap years.

Q: Why are birthdays good for you?

A: People who have the most birthdays live the longest.

Teacher: When's your birthday?

Pupil: July 23rd.

Teacher: What year?

Pupil: Every year.

Q: Why was the baby strawberry crying?

A: Because its parents were in a jam.

Q: What do you call babies in the army?

A: Infantry!

32. Q: What's the only kind of cake left when you're the last one to arrive at the party?

A: Choco-late cake!

Q: What did the cow want for her birthday?

A:  A trip to the moo-vies!

Q: Why did the boy toss his cake across the room?

A: Because he wanted to "throw" a party!

Q: What did the snowman want on his cake?

A: Extra frosting!

Q: What does a cat eat on its birthday?

A: Cake and mice cream

Q: Where do you find a birthday present for a cat?

A: In a cat-alog!

Q: What is your favorite type of present?

A: Another present!

Q: What did the birthday balloon say to the pin?

A: "Hi, Buster."

Knock knock.
**Who's there?**
Sue!
**Sue who?**
Sue-prise, Sue-prise, it's your birthday!

Q: What did the bald guy say when he was given a comb for his birthday?

A: "Thanks! I'll never part with it."

Knock Knock.
**Who's there?**
Manny!
**Manny who?**
Manny happy returns of the day!

Knock, knock!
**Who's there?**
Osborn!
**Osborn who?**
Osborn today; let's celebrate my birthday!

Q: What do you sing to a cow on its birthday?

A: Happy birthday to moo!

Q: What do rabbits play at birthday parties?

A: Musical hares!

Q: What do you buy an elephant for its birthday?

A: A trunk-ful of presents!

Q: Why did the girl feel warm on her birthday?

A: Because people kept toasting her

Q: What did the children say to the sad elephant on its birthday?

A: Don't worry! Age is ir-elephant!

Q: When is a golf ball like a birthday cake?

A: When it's sliced

Knock Knock!
Who's there?
Bacon.
Bacon who?
Bacon a cake for your birthday!

# BONUS *Jokes*

Below are bonus jokes. Do you feel special?!

## WISE DINOSAUR JOKES

These are the type of joke that allows a child to get some funny advice or words of wisdom from Dino, one of the most intelligent, dangerous, and hilarious animals in the universe. Below is the list of wise dinosaur jokes to crack your kids' ribs with:

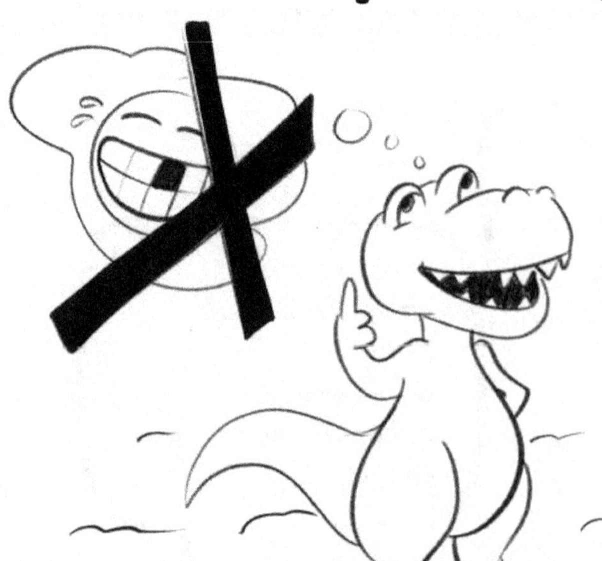

Can I get a word of wisdom, Dino?

Of course!

When your mom is mad at your dad, don't let her brush your hair.

Can I get a word of wisdom, Dino?

Of course!

Don't pick on your sister when she's holding a baseball bat.

Can I get a word of wisdom, Dino?

Of course!

Never trust a dog to watch your food.

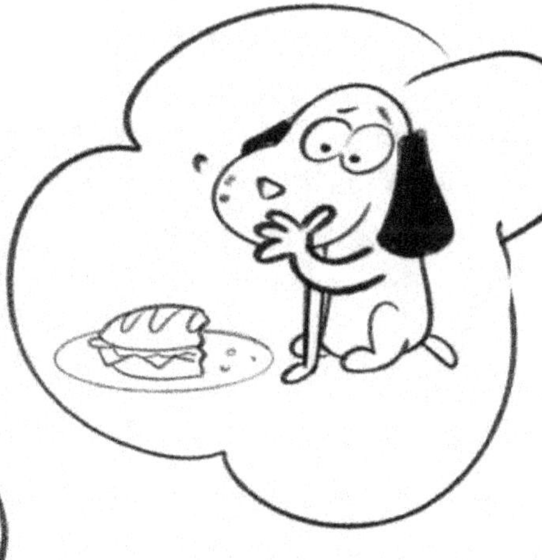

Can I get a word of wisdom, Dino?

Of course!

Never try to baptize a cat.

Can I get a word of wisdom, Dino?

Of course!

Don't ask your mom for anything if you didn't wash the dishes when she asked you to.

Can I get a word of wisdom, Dino?

Of course!

When you get a bad grade in school, show it to your mom when she's on the phone.

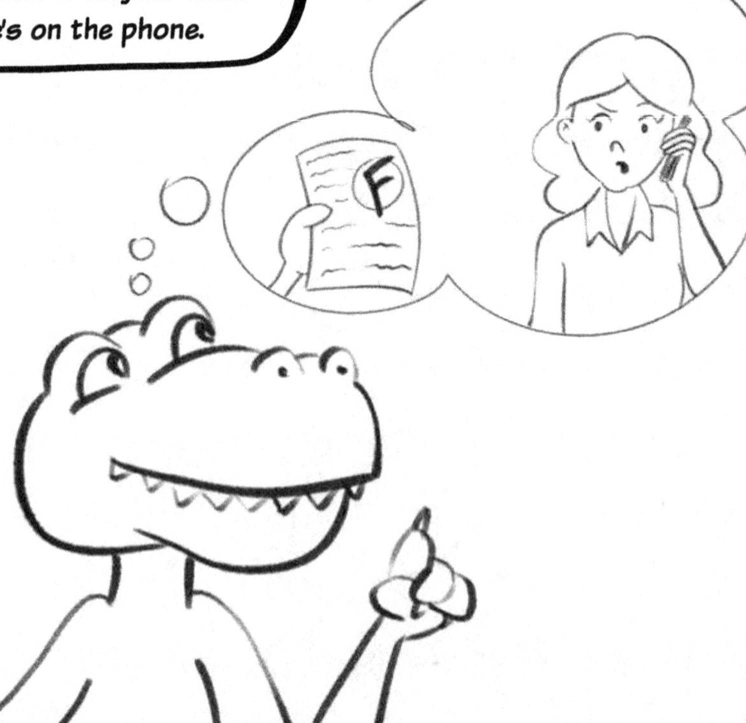

# RIDDLES

Do you love confusing your friends but making them laugh at the same time? We've got some of the funniest, most bizarre riddles that will leave your friends and family scratching their heads and slapping their knees.

Q: What do you have to break before you can use it?

A: An **egg**.

Q: I'm long when I'm young and short when I'm old. What am I?

A: A candle.

Q: What question can you never say 'yes' to?

A: Are you asleep?

Q: Which month has 28 days?

A: All of them.

Q: What holds water but is full of holes?

A: A sponge.

Q: There is a one-story house where everything is red. Red doors, red walls, red furniture. What color are the stairs?

A: There are no stairs. It's a one-story house.

Q: What can't you see but is always in front of you?

A: The future.

Q: What goes up but never down?

A: Your age.

Q: What gets wet when it dries?

A: A towel.

Q: What do you keep after giving it to someone?

A: Your word.

Q: How can a plane fly if there isn't a single person on board?

A: Everyone onboard is married.

Q: A room contains a candle, a fireplace, a kerosene lamp, and a match. What do you light first?

A: The match.

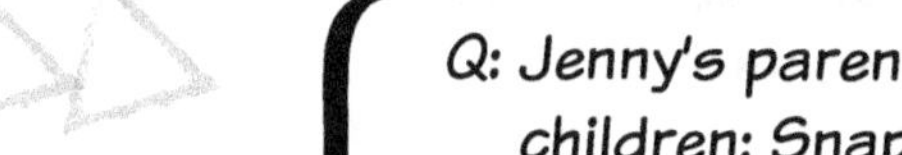


Q: The more of it there is, the less you see. What is it?
A: Darkness.

Q: Jenny's parents have three children: Snap, Crackle, and...?
A: Jenny.

Q: What doesn't talk but replies to you?
A: Your echo.


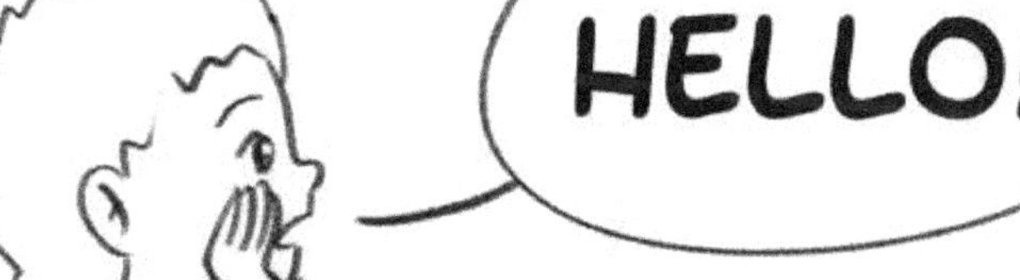


HELLO!


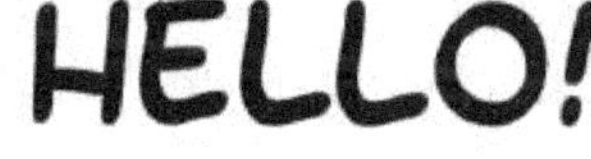


HELLO!

Q: What has 88 keys but can't open any locks?

A: A piano.

Q: What's something that's extremely light but can't be held for more than five minutes?

A: Your breath.

Q: If you share me, you haven't kept me, and if you've got me, you want to share me. What am I?

A: A secret.

Q: What can't you put in a pot?

A: Its lid.

Q: I am yours, but other people use me more than you do. What am I?

A: Your name.

Q: What has an eye but can't see?

A: A needle.

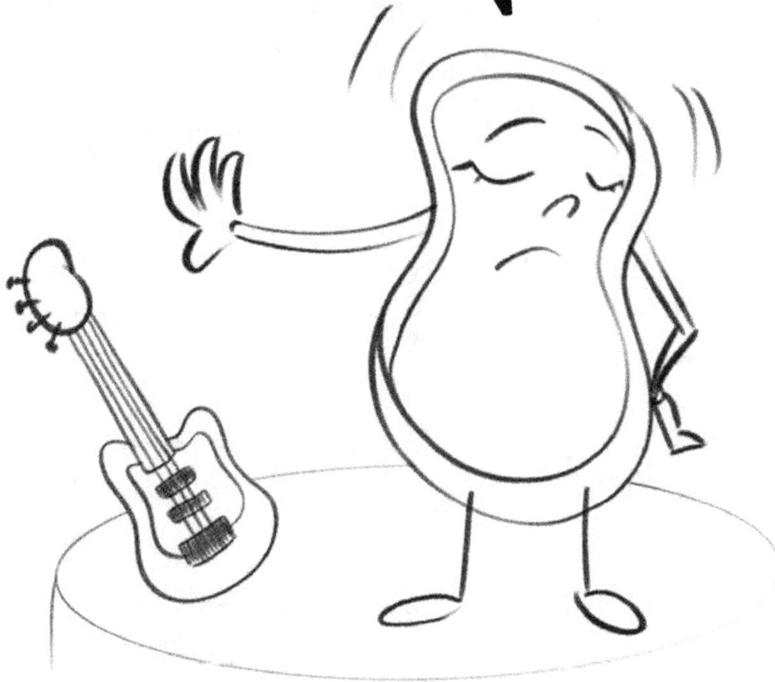
Q: What has many needles but can't sew?
A: A pine tree.
Q: What has hands and a face but can't clap or smile?
A: A clock.
Q: What has four legs, one foot, and one head?
A: A Bed.
Q: What band doesn't play music?
A: A rubber band.

Q: What has many teeth but no mouth?

A: A comb.

Q: What never speaks but has many words?

A: Books.

Q: What goes around the world but never leaves a corner?

A: Stamps.

Q: What has four fingers and a thumb but is not a hand?

A: A glove.

Q: Where do walls meet?

A: In corners.

Q: What coat do you put on wet?

A: Paint.

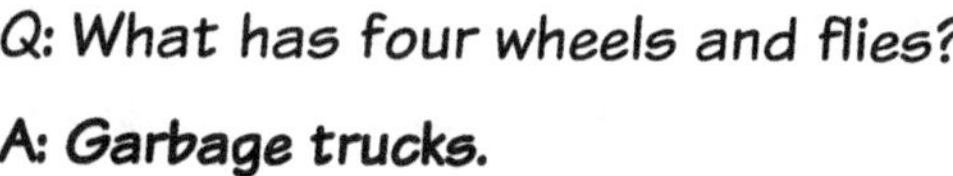


Q: I'm an odd number. Remove a letter, and I become even. What number am I?

A: Seven.

Q: I am a five-letter word that becomes shorter when you add two letters. What word am I?

A: Short.

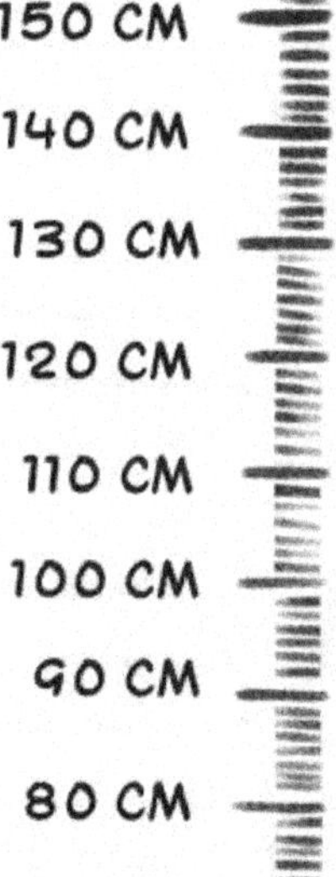


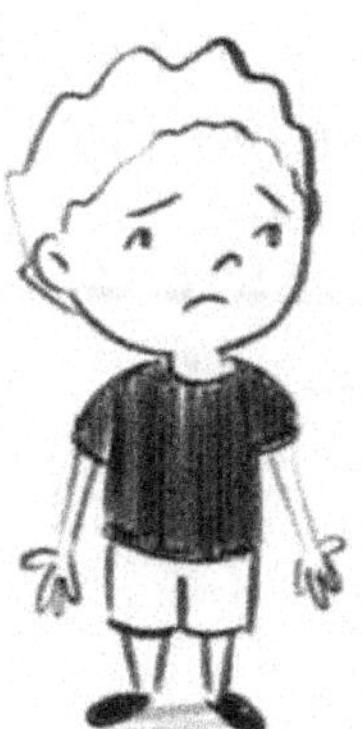

Q: I'm seen once in June, twice in November, three times in December, but not once in August. What am I?

A: The letter 'e'.

Q: What starts with 'e' and only contains a single letter?

A: An envelope.

Q: When I'm forward, I'm heavy; when I'm backward, I'm not. What am I?

A: The word 'not'.

Q: What five-letter word is pronounced the same even when you take away four letters?

A: Queue.

Q: What will you find at the end of everything?

A: The letter 'g'.

Q: What has a mouth but never talks, can run but never walks, has a bed but doesn't sleep, and has a head but never weeps?

A: A river.

Q: What takes up no space but can still fill a room?

A: Light.

# PUNS

Sometimes, the best way to be funny is to keep it simple. Take a look at these simple yet hilarious puns.

What concert costs 45 cents? A 50 Cent concert opened by Nickelback.

Time flies like an arrow. Fruit flies like an apple.

What did the grape say when it was squashed? Nothing, it just let out a little wine.

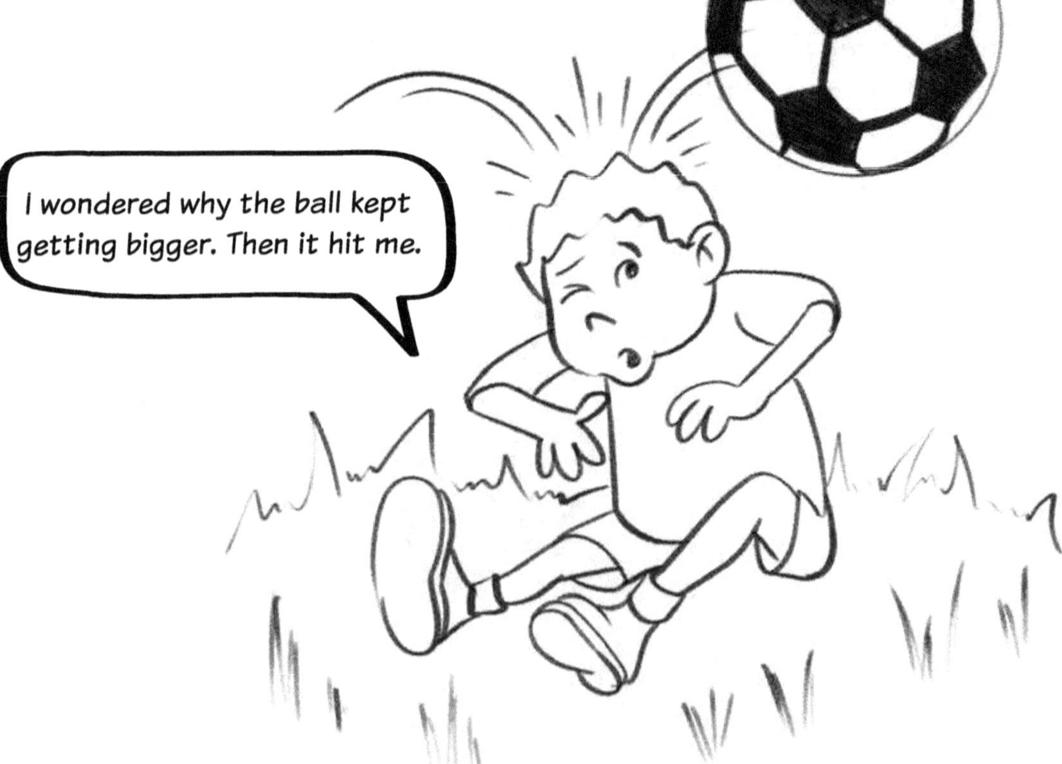
I dreamt that I was swimming in orange soda last night. Too bad it was just a Fanta sea.

Geology rocks, but geography is where it's at.

If you need an ark to save two of every animal, call me. I Noah guy.

I wondered why the ball kept getting bigger. Then it hit me.

I've got a heart of a lion and a lifetime ban from the zoo.

You can't trust atoms. They make up everything.

Waking up from my nap was a real eye-opener.

To the person who invented zero: thanks for nothing!

My candy cane collection is in mint condition.

It would be so uplifting to be able to fly.

# CONCLUSION

There you have it, kids! All the jokes you'll ever need to have your friends and family crying with laughter for years to come. We hope that you loved reading and telling these jokes as much as we loved putting them together. Now go out there and get cracking – there's laughter to be heard and fun to be had!